WOODSTOCK

an

Archaeological

Mystery

LESLEY FEAKES

Published by Geerings of Ashford Ltd.

Published by Geerings of Ashford Ltd., Cobbs Wood House, Chart Road, Ashford, Kent TN23 1EP.
Tel (01233) 633366   Fax (01233) 639404

1st Edition 2001

© Text copyright Lesley Feakes including all pictures, photographs and diagrams unless otherwise acknowledged and credited.

Design and printing by Geerings of Ashford Ltd.

ISBN 1 873953 33 X

Acknowledgments:-

Firstly thanks are due to Garth and Edmund Doubleday (G. H. Dean & Co.) owners of Highsted Farm, without who's co-operation and interest the archaeological investigation would not have been possible.

Also, thanks to Lord Kingsdown and John Leigh-Pemberton for permission to walk their land and record some of the features (e.g. in Wychling Wood).

I am grateful to Oliver Rackham for his permission (and that of his publisher J. M. Dent & Sons) to use the map of Devon reaves and to quote from his book "The History of the Countryside". He also very kindly read through chapter 4 and gave me a few hints (I cannot be sure that I followed them all!)

I would like to thank all the enthusiastic members of Maidstone, Lower Medway, Thanet and a few from Hastings Archaeological Groups who took part in the digs. Special thanks to Clare Curran, Beena Patel, Alastair Hawkins, and David Cox, who were the main excavation leaders.

David Rudling (Field Archaeological Unit, University College London) needs mentioning and thanking because it was he that has taught me so much, made the subject so interesting and fun to do and was sympathetic to my more 'unusual' ideas. He is always willing to listen to everyone!

Thanks to Dr. David Perkins and Len Jay (now sadly deceased) of the Thanet Trust for Archaeology who gave us quiet encouragement for our digs. To John Dove, pottery expert without equal, from Eastbourne, who was so helpful and knowledgeable in identifying even small scraps of pots! Thanks also to Nigel MacPherson-Grant who pointed us in the right direction as to how to spot those sherds!

Eric Goldsmith, who was so knowledgeable on Rodmersham and who drew the sedilia on page 66. Thanks to Arthur Page who very kindly allowed me to print his 1955 photographs of Highsted graves and to Peter Barker for the photograph of the gold staters.

Two physicists who gave me encouragement:- Alister Bartlett who did such a good job in the geophysical survey and who sent me information on the Nazca Plains when I told him of my observations in Kent. He did not disbelieve me at all, just added that it would be rather difficult to categorically prove things! Secondly, Ian Oliver, who I taught with for nearly ten years and who was so helpful and inspirational in teaching physics. He was the one who first insisted that I should carry my theories further and write a book!

Finally to Alison and Peter Hawkins who have been such good friends with so much enthusiasm, ideas and support. Alison of course being the one who originally found the site and who knew and gleaned so much information from local people. I only hope those local people enjoy their book!

Lesley Feakes 30.8.01

All rights reserved. No part of this publication may be reproduced, stored in a retrieval system or transmitted, in any form or by any means, electronic, mechanical, photocopying, recording or otherwise, without the prior permission of the Copyright owners.

WOODSTOCK

LESLEY FEAKES

Best wishes from Lesley Feakes
24.4.02

Bronze Age Loop and Socket Axe found in 1928

To Tunstall
To Sittingbourne
Ruins Barn Road

QUARRY III

Grid North

QUARRY II

Position of I.A. graves found in 1955

Main Bank

Position of ditch - now filled

Highsted 23.9.98

Square slightly sunken orchard

Banks - now largely flattened

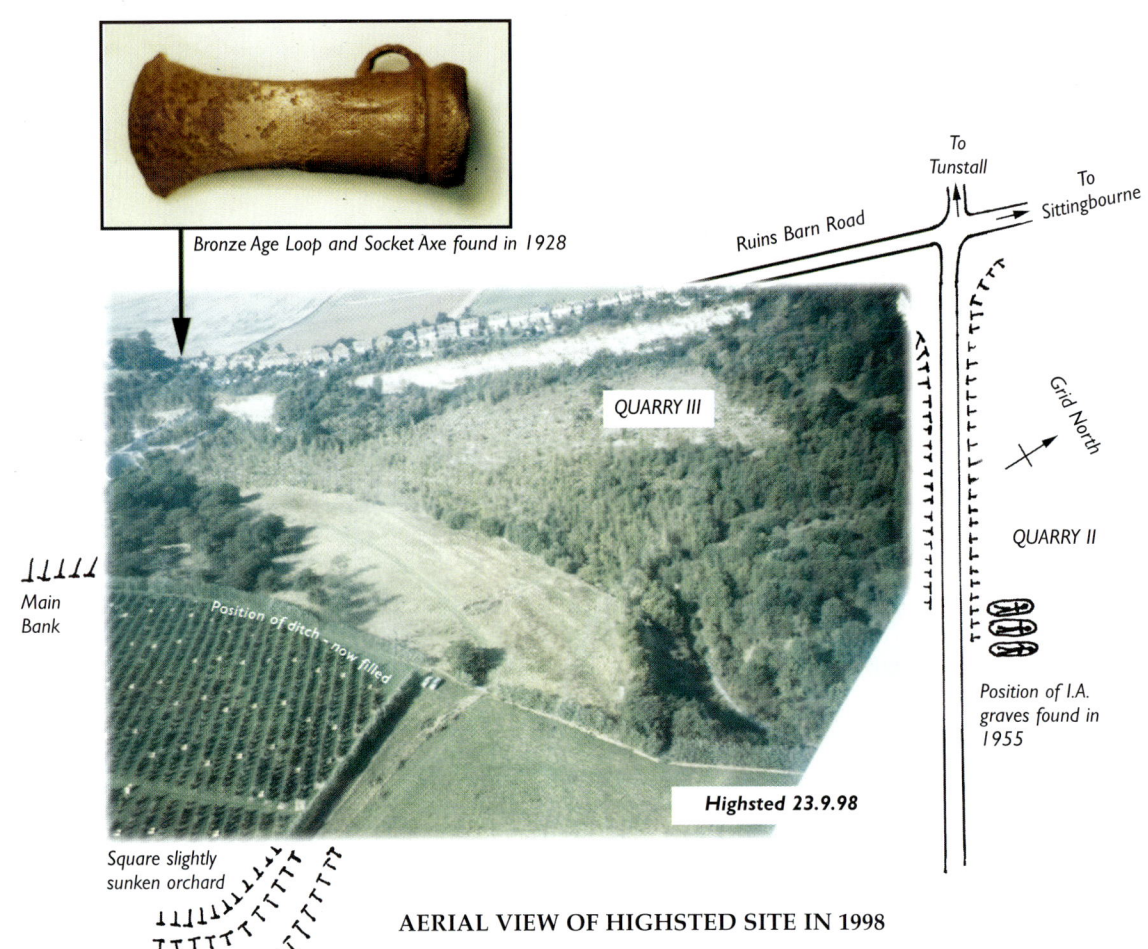

AERIAL VIEW OF HIGHSTED SITE IN 1998

Looking due south towards Woodstock
Note:-
Brown tall growth marks position of the ditches (possibly 3). Green short growth is over the line of the flint banks. Dark horseshoe is a patch of thistles! green lane to the left of that is a farm track.

Highsted 23.9.98

Contents

SECTION I :- Site, investigations, digs and assessment = the straight archaeology !

Chapter 1 :- Global Position 9
"Men move boundary stones" NIV.   Job 24: v.2
"Some remove the landmarks" A.V.

Chapter 2 :- The Chalk Cemetery 15
"Tis a chequer board of nights and days
Where destiny with men for pieces plays
.....and one by one back in the closet lays"
Rubaiyat of Omar Khayyam

Chapter 3 :- Early Investigations, 1985 - 1995 21
"Till now the doubtful dusk revealed
The knolls once more where, couch'd at ease
The white kine glimmer'd and the trees
Laid their dark arms about the field."
Tennyson

Chapter 4 :- Trackways and Waterways 29
"Stand at the crossroads and look; ask for the ancient paths,
ask where the good way is and walk in it......."
Jeremiah 6, v.16

Chapter 5 :- "Wool Over One's Eyes" 41
He thought he saw a bank of sand
With nought but rocks and ferns
He looked again and found it was
A pile of Belgic urns!
---with apologies to Lewis Carroll.

Chapter 6 :- The First Dig , 1996 47
"And see you marks that show and fade,
like shadows on the Downs ?
O they are the lines the Flint Men made,
To guard their wondrous towns."
Puck's song by Rudyard Kipling

Chapter 7 :- The Second Dig, 1998. 53
"Earth feet, loam feet lifted in country mirth
Mirth of those long since under the earth."
T.S.Eliot

Chapter 8 :- Assessment, Mystery Solved ? 57
"Under the days declining beam and call
Images and memories from ruin or from ancient trees
For I would ask a question of them all"
W.B.Yeats

SECTION II :- Wildlife, wider views, and lateral thinking !

Chapter 9 :- The Chalk Pit Eden, and Other Wildlife 61

"How pleasant thy banks and green valley below,
Where wild in the woodlands the primroses grow."
R.Burns

Chapter 10 :- Into the Fringe 73

"And time can crumble all but cannot touch
The book that burns faster than we can read"
Michael Roberts

Chapter 11 :- The People who Walked Straight 79

"But my Totem saw the shame ; from his ridge-pole shrine he came,
And he told me in a vision of the night:-
'There are nine and sixty ways of constructing tribal lays
'And every single one of them is right !'
Rudyard Kipling 'In the Neolithic Age'.

Chapter 12 :- Beyond the Pale 87

"Mock on , mock on; 'tis all in vain
You throw the sand against the wind
And the wind blows it back again"
William Blake.

Chapter 13 :- The Horse of the Hesperis 95

"Time present and time past
Are both perhaps present in time future
And time future contained in time past,
If all time is eternally present
All time is unredeemable."
T.S.Eliot

Chapter 14 Circles of the Mind 101

"And the Windmill sails are turning like a wheel within a wheel…"

Chapter 15:- Hints and Advice for Young (and old) Time Trackers 107

"Dig and delve in your own backyard
For buckles and bobbins, coin or shard
Bottles and pipes and bones of old
One Man's rubbish is another one's gold!"

Chapter 16:- Afterthoughts or the Eadish 113

"Is it illusion? Or does there a spirit from perfecter ages,
Here, even yet, amid change, and corruption, abide?
Is it illusion that lures the barbarian stranger,
Brings him with gold to the shrine, brings him in arms to the gate?"
Arthur Hugh Clough

Further Reading 119

Index 121

WOODSTOCK

an Archaeological Mystery.

An account of the HIGHSTED/WOODSTOCK prehistoric multiphase site near Sittingbourne, Kent.

by

LESLEY FEAKES

Preface

Since late 1985 I have known that a previously uninvestigated, unrecorded, ancient site lay hidden under the small ancient woodland of Highsted, near Sittingbourne. This is an account of my findings since then. Hopefully my writing falls within the accepted constraints of an accurate archaeological account but is aimed primarily as a 'readable' book for the general public. A general public now turned on by television programmes such as "Time Team" ...keen to take part in archaeology but not realising that there are many, many sites in rural areas (particularly in Kent) that have never been even noticed by main stream archaeologists. I will hasten to add that all investigations (even just walking a field) must always be with the co-operation and goodwill of the landowner. On that score, I have been extremely fortunate in that the Doubleday family (who own Highsted) have known me as a local farmer's daughter since 1950. It is with their kind permission that these investigations have all been carried out. The site is visible across the valley from our family squash club, on the site of Oak Tree Farm, but it was the discovery of 26 Iron Age graves in the Highsted chalk pit in 1955 that triggered the interest of all the villagers. We had our own "Time Team" investigation way back then! My brother David, then 15, was asked to help trowel the site ...I was **most** disappointed that I was not asked ...but presumed in those days (rightly or wrongly) that it was because I was a girl and perhaps too young.

What I always think is tremendous is that it was a very observant mechanical-shovel operator Archie Pack, who noticed a skull roll out and stopped his machine in time and enabled them to rescue the further 25 graves. How many other graves or funerary urns had been destroyed unnoticed in previous years we shall never know, some were recorded and some were not. We know that when they first dug the chalk by hand after the First World War (around 1920) a *'Horse and cart'*, *'complete with its trappings'* and in one verbal account *'with a soldier'* was found. At least three Rodmersham villagers (now deceased) had told us of this find. We were told that *'an account and pictures were published in the local newspaper'*. But my scouring of both the 'East Kent Gazette' and the 'Kent Messenger', have drawn blanks. There you are! ...all the budding young "Time Team" enthusiasts ...research the possibility ...if you find the reference it will possibly be the first such Iron Age find outside Yorkshire and you will get the accolade of 'finding' it! (I am guessing on I.A. as that seems to fit best with the descriptions we have been given.)

But what followed the 1955 excavation? The archaeologists involved on the dig were so alarmed that *'things would be stolen'* that we were asked to keep it hush-hush until everything was rescued. Then what happened? All the artifacts and notes were stolen from the site hut! The archaeologists died within the year and the account was never written! This intriguing 'Archaeological who-dun-it' points to an inside job ...but read the account as published in *Archaeologia Cantiana* in 1978, printed in Chapter 2. Do some of the pieces of pottery (sherds) we found in 1996 match the *'missing pots'* that are in Edinburgh Museum? Is the *'Beaker'* held by the mysterious *'pot-donator'* an ancient corded Bronze Age Beaker ...does it match the piece we have found? A huge pity is that elderly archaeologists with private collections often neglect to will their unique local pieces to a museum that would recognise their importance. There is a gap in Beaker finds. They are recorded in the Medway towns and in Thanet but nothing at all in the Sittingbourne area! Read on to decide for yourselves, if Highsted was a possible multiphase settlement ...a settlement area for all the people buried in the chalk pit. If one had stood them up they would have been facing home ......

I would like to say here also that the real discoverer of the Highsted site is my friend Alison Hawkins (née Young) we walked the site together in 1985. Both she and I have long ancestral roots in the area (mine is through my great grandmother) and we both trace back to the village of Newnham some six miles from Highsted. We would also like to thank Len Jay, now sadly dead, an archaeologist of Thanet Trust who always gave us the support and encouragement we needed in trying to work out the archaeological possibilities of Highsted.

I have named it WOODSTOCK because that is what the whole area was called when Woodstock house existed. Many people may have dismissed the banks as being part of the estate ....and that may be why they may have omitted to recognise the earthworks for what they really are. One only has to read the account of George Payne removing the tumulus S.E. of Woodstock house ..... *'till it was a hole'* to realise how much of the ancient archaeology of the area has been needlessly destroyed. Look at all the sarsen stones marked on older maps (see Chapter 14) ...now all gone or moved ....did they once stand on 'reave' lines, possible Bronze Age divisions as in Devon? It sometimes requires a different way of looking at things to realise the truth. I have been told quite a few inaccuracies over the years by archaeologists who are so determined that they are right e.g. *"There are no defensive I.A. sites in Kent bar Bigbury and Oldbury"* ......have people been looking for the wrong clues? Woodland was (and is) a feature of Kent; were sites defended with massive wooden ramparts? Was the old name of 'Woodstock' a memory of a *very* old site ...predating any Saxon settlements; did it have a stockade ...like Stockbury, and perhaps Timbold Hill (Timber-old hill?), Pitstock (two in the area) and Bistock?*

Throughout the years I have had considerable static, scoffing and cold-shouldering from certain established Kent archaeologists and I do so hope that keen young archaeologists meet a much more encouraging climate than I have had to contend with. Despite sending accounts in to the County Archaeology department, nothing about Highsted has appeared on the Sites and Monuments record so far (as far as I know).

As there seems to be no local Kent Journal willing to publish my findings in this more informal format, I am writing this book and publishing it myself. Perhaps I have not established enough real evidence, perhaps my theories are *"too theoretical"* as some who think they 'know' all about Kent's archaeology have professed...but on the other hand I could be right: and I leave the true solving of the mysteries ...to the reader!

Although the established archaeology world might find fault with my writing (a late Kent Archaeological Society senior member wrote and told me I wrote like a *'beginner'* and implied my archaeological drawings were *'not up to standard'*) the KAS attitude and general encouragement to members has now improved no end! Also I feel it would be unfair on the local people, especially of Rodmersham, if I did not record my findings so far achieved, for I know they are very interested in the local history. (See their excellent Millennium publication on Rodmersham published by the Parish Council in A.D. 2000).

There is a short report I wrote on Highsted in 1996 that is lodged in Sittingbourne Library.

I leave it to others to extend the investigation of the site of Highsted/Woodstock if they wish and prove or disprove anything that I have written. My paintings in some cases are with artistic licence but the finds drawings are all as accurate as I could make them and there are many photographs that I have taken over the years.

It is plain to me that there is an enormous amount of ancient, prehistoric archaeology to be noticed, recorded and investigated in Kent. **Why it has been ignored for so long ....is the biggest mystery of all!** There is no end of archaeology in all counties that is slowly being eroded by the plough and there is an enormous gap in research/practical archaeology (field walking and observation) that could be filled by keen volunteers. It is an enormous pity that there is no central archaeological unit in Kent to investigate more sites and to tender for construction surveys. I can only hope that what I have written in this book might prompt the county to fill the void in some way and organize a Trust for archaeology much on the lines of Canterbury Archaeology Trust and Thanet Trust for Archaeology that are doing such good work in their respective areas. We perhaps have the greatest amount of prehistory of all the Home Counties (as many barrows as in Wiltshire) yet we seem to have done the least about investigating it and are content to let it be ploughed away; and because some has already been ploughed away are content to presume that it was never there at all!

There has been criticism that I write with too many question marks!

But there are reasons behind my style that suggest I should keep them in. The questions are posed primarily because I would like people to think laterally. I may have raised ideas that they had never even thought of before. Additionally, the theories I have put forward are not necessarily valid; I am tentatively suggesting they <u>might</u> be and that they would warrant further investigation. Sometimes there are too many variables that might prohibit categorical proof.... but perhaps people may come up with more information that then narrows those variables. Finally, I have taught Science in British secondary schools and with the National Curriculum one has to pose questions and continually encourage pupils to ask questions themselves with the aim of solving them.... I suppose I now find it difficult getting out of the habit! There may not be answers to some of the questions at present, all the more reason to query!

For instance it is even possible that Kent's gravel bottomed river valleys e.g. Highsted and Doddington, nurtured some of the oldest inhabitants of our Country .....and no one has even bothered to look! Yet there are easily accessible, disused, gravel pits just waiting for some keen palaeontologist of the future to trowel back the past and discover a 50,000 year old *Highsted* inhabitant or even the original…..*Dodman*.

*Generally speaking my reference for name meanings has been "Kentish Place Names" and "The Place Names of Kent" by J. K. Wallenberg, but as the real meanings are often lost in the past I have sometimes used educated guesses where the meaning could be interpreted differently and he has overlooked that possibility. e.g. the enigma of Trosley (Trottiscliffe) he completely omits.

Plan of WOODSTOCK/HIGHSTED Iron Age/ multiphase site near Sittingbourne, Kent

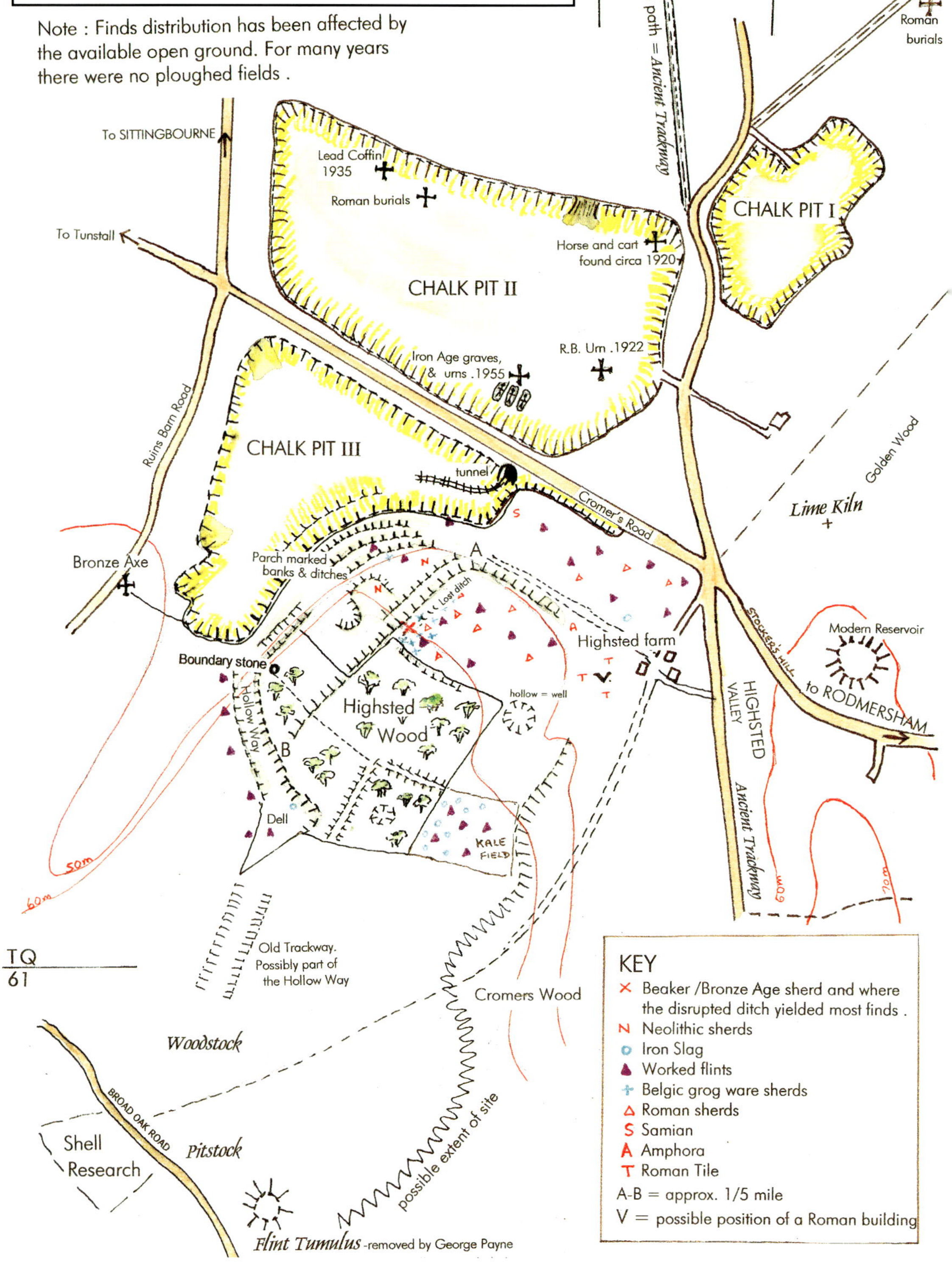

Section 1-

Chapter 1
Global Position

There is only one Highsted in Kent .

Granted, there is a Highstead and the spelling with an 'a' is likely a variation of the same name meaning, 'a high place'. Highstead is near Chislet, N.E. of Canterbury and Canterbury Archaeological Trust have investigated and recorded the Bronze Age/Iron Age finds in their Journal (see 'Canterbury's Archaeology'1990.)

"Men move boundary stones" N.I.V. Job 24 :v. 2
"Some remove the land marks". A.V.

So to avoid any confusion I have used the name 'WOODSTOCK' for my book. As you will see on the estate map, Highsted Wood (where the main part of the site lies) is distinctly included as Woodstock. So was the name invented for the estate or did it exist long before that? I think the latter. But the fact that the banks and ditches fall within the estate and constitute much of the wooded area may well have been the reason archaeologists have ignored, discounted or simply not noticed that the earthworks are indeed, ancient.

There is only one Woodstock in Kent also! Whatever the original name of the wooden stockade was ...is anyone's guess.....but see later in Chapter 10.

The access track to the site most likely joined what is now Broad Oak Road so again, where ones gate is, is one's address = Woodstock.

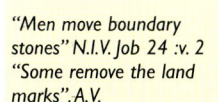

A photograph of Woodstock House (now demolished)

"WOODSTOCK HOUSE"

There is a modern method of fixing the exact spot in the world I am talking about. The Global Positioning System (GPS) using a hand held instrument that bounces a signal off satellites has been employed to give readers the location of this site. The boundary stones (ancient ones) have long been removed but the Victorians left us a Parish Boundary stone that does the job just as well and the reading at that point is: 53. 19. 18. North and 00. 43. 79 East.

I would have liked to have used the nearest sarsen but that seems to be impossible as it was lost in the chalk pit (see 1909 map).

A a photograph of my daughter Sunita, and Elinor Hawkins, 'discovering' the Victorian stone in Highsted Wood in 1985. It has not changed much in the last 15 years except the coppice stool has forced it over a little more as you can see in this recent picture. The "T" is on the north side and denotes the parish of Tunstall and the other side bears an "S" for Sittingbourne. It is marked as BS = Boundary Stone on the 1909 map (just after the last "L" of Tunstall).

1909 Map of Woodstock.
Scale:- 6cm = 1km.

In addition to the site plan that I have drawn, there is an aerial photograph to help you understand the site (frontispiece). The chalk pit loses its depth from the air but you can distinctly see its edges and the houses on Ruins Barn Road. It is as well to compare that aerial with the Ordnance Survey map. The *'burial ground'* marked in the middle chalk pit is in fact an illusion as it is a point some 100 metres in mid air, for the chalk the graves were found in has long been ground into cement!

I have included this modern section of Ordnance Survey Map so that you can now relate everything together. On some of the older O.S. maps the 'avenue' across the Woodstock estate is shown. This avenue (probably confluent with the hollow way) does not make a lot of sense as an access road to the house but it would make sense as an older hollow way connecting to Broad Oak Lane. (See chapter 4) However, was the feature used as a 'ladies walk-way'? More research is needed ....for anyone interested .

Note the older map also shows that the home farm of Woodstock estate was called Pitstock. That name is only used now for Pitstock Farm in Rodmersham parish. That farm has evidence of a Roman Villa/Farm, showing on an old RAF aerial photograph. I have walked the footpath, picked up tile and a piece of

Note: mistakes on maps do still occur :-
1. Look again at the modern printed O.S. section shown. Locals of Rodmersham and Highsted have always called the lower Highsted Valley road 'Pond Bottom Road'. Pond Bottom itself is where the road eventually forks to Frinsted and Wormshill. On the old estate maps it is 'Long Bottom'...easily equatable to Pond Bottom. BUT it is always that way around! It is not, according to the locals, 'Bottom Pond'! Now someone has mistakenly put it down as 'Barton Pond'!
2. Cheney Hill always was to us locals, the road to Milstead from Highsted valley. It is not (according to our Oak Tree Farm tithe map) the fenced footpath alongside Shoulder-o-Mutton wood bordering the north of the farm. However, it is a pity the name of 'Giddyhorn' has been lost ...perhaps someone changed it to Cheney?
3. 'Brownings Farm cottages' are in fact Bridges Farm Cottages (See Rodmersham's millennium booklet .)
I have informed the O.S. of the mistakes and hopefully they will correct them in the next edition.
What is also very sad, are the number of footpaths we have lost in the Rodmersham area that were so clearly marked on 1909 maps.

Modern O.S map.
Scale 6cm = 1km.

Reproduced from the Ordnance Survey on behalf of the Controller of Her Majesty's Stationery Office, Crown Copyright MC100033282.

11

I.A. Graves, 1955

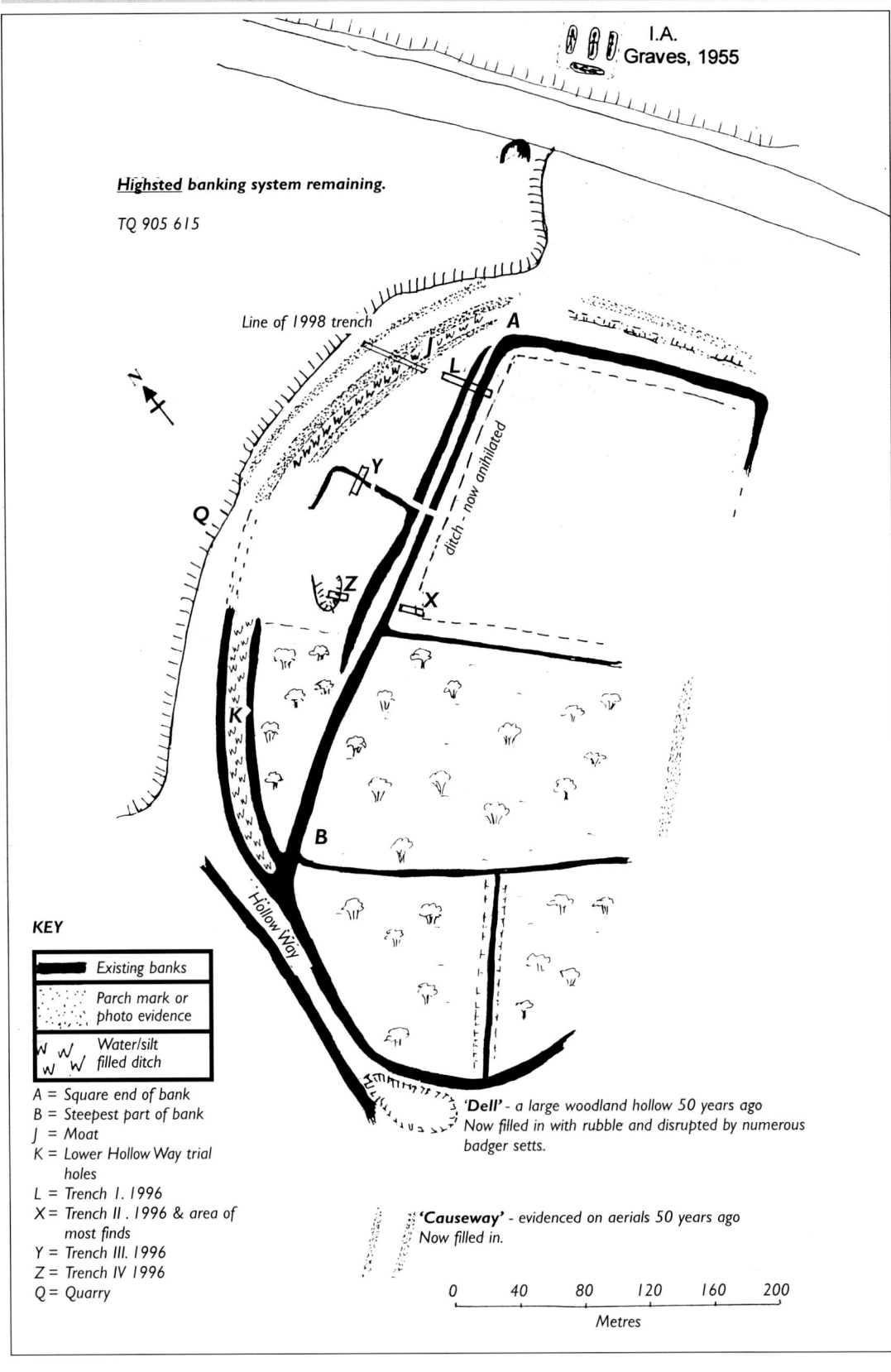

Highsted banking system remaining.

TQ 905 615

Line of 1998 trench

ditch - now anihilated

KEY

- Existing banks
- Parch mark or photo evidence
- Water/silt filled ditch

A = Square end of bank
B = Steepest part of bank
J = Moat
K = Lower Hollow Way trial holes
L = Trench I. 1996
X = Trench II. 1996 & area of most finds
Y = Trench III. 1996
Z = Trench IV 1996
Q = Quarry

'**Dell**' - a large woodland hollow 50 years ago Now filled in with rubble and disrupted by numerous badger setts.

'**Causeway**' - evidenced on aerials 50 years ago Now filled in.

0   40   80   120   160   200
Metres

Hollow Way

12

amphora (Roman wine storage jar) and informed the farmer who owns it ...so sites abound for interested researchers! But budding young archaeologists **must** get permission from the landowners! (Hope you have read my preface and read Chapter 15).

In 1891, George Payne F.S.A., the noted archaeologist who recorded so much in and around Sittingbourne, was asked to remove a 'Tumulus' from the Woodstock estate by the then owner Mr. Twopenny. George Payne removed it till it was a hole instead of a bump! He did not find evidence of a burial and the entire mound was made of flint. The location was 'S.E. of Woodstock House' and despite researching his notes (lodged in the Guild Hall Museum, Rochester) I cannot find any closer reference. Studying the map it looks as if the circle of trees marked is the spot.

In addition to the maps already shown here is a diagrammatic plan of the banking system which might help readers to see it does look like more classic planes of Iron Age camps although the southern and eastern areas are badly damaged and lost.

Finally, here is a location map to show whereabouts the site is in the County of Kent.

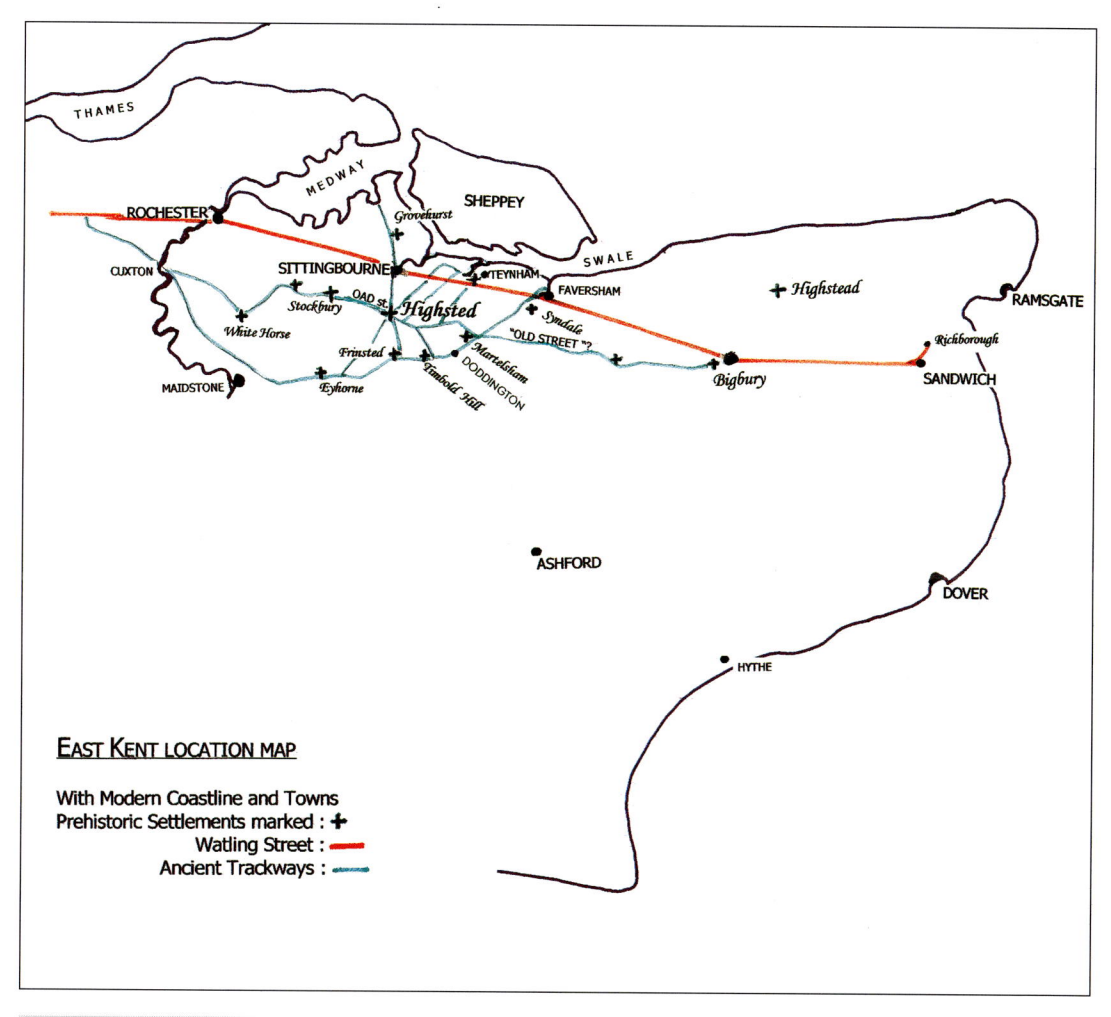

East Kent Location Map

With Modern Coastline and Towns
Prehistoric Settlements marked : +
Watling Street : ▬
Ancient Trackways : ▬▬

Curiously the location considered in this next chapter no longer exists!
It is a point in time and space suspended some 10 metres above the floor of the Chalk Pit!

Sacred Oak/Mistletoe Grove in the Highsted valley, early Iron age.
Burial places probably remained for millenia. Snakes were a symbol of rebirth **not** of evil.
It would make sense to suppose that death gave rise to life...... hence the snakes and oaks with mistletoe atop the older barrows.
Light and darkness, sun and moon ..... All is conjecture based on facts ...... All have many echos in other religions, Essenes, Hinduism, Minoan etc.
Many people feel the beauty, peace and closeness to God in cathedrals of living trees. It is absurd to suppose that only 'learned men' have clues to the distant past.... we all may have faint ancestral 'memories' to our own inherent spirituality....

"The bell that rings inside your mind is challenging the doors of Time...."
"Magic" Freddie Mercury.

Chapter 2

The Chalk Cemetery

In 1955 Rodmersham and Highsted residents were excited by a "Time Team" type excavation right on their doorstep. The Town Clerk of Sittingbourne, Don Allen, lived in Rodmersham and local boys were asked if they would like to help with the dig. My brother David was one of those so I had a first hand account given to me every evening as to what was being found. I was envious that I was not asked to help as well, and at the time ...thought that was, perhaps, that I was a girl!

> "Tis a chequer board of nights and days
> Where destiny with men for pieces plays
> ....and one by one back in the closet lays."
> Rubaiyat of Omar Khayyam

Although at first it was supposed the graves might be Beaker folk it was quickly established they were Iron Age. Why that word 'Beaker' hung in my mind I do not know but I am sure in retrospect that it was mentioned.

The most remarkable thing was that there were funerary urns (cremations) and interments on the same site. Whether the burials were dug in over the top of an existing cremation site is still unclear ....because all the artefacts and notes were stolen from the site hut. Stolen right at the end of the dig when they were already crated up ready for despatch to a museum ....but they never got there! Read this 1978 report from the "Archaeologia Cantiana" published by the Kent Archaeological Society and written by David Kelly:-

"In 1955 it was reported that an emergency excavation of a late Celtic cemetery had been undertaken at Highsted on land belonging to A.P.C.M. Ltd., and that a report would be published. The pottery was brought to Maidstone Museum by the archaeological assistant at that time, but, together with the drawings had to be returned and was subsequently stolen, so that no report was published or is likely to be.

(printed here with K.A.S. permission)

The cemetery was discovered during the extension of the A.P.C.M. chalk quarry and the approximate grid reference is TQ 908618. The only record of the excavation in the Museum is a set of six photographs presented by the late Mr. A. N. Berry, of Tunstall, who took part in the excavation. One shows a number of graves, some still containing inhumation burials, and the others individual graves with pots accompanying the skeletons. Mr. Berry stated that there were twenty inhumation and six cremation burials, with Belgic pottery and a La Tene (presumably III) brooch. Such pottery as is clearly identifiable in the photographs is Belgic: two small bowls with 'S' profile and a single cordon below the neck and a narrow-mouthed globular jar. In September, 1977, Miss Helen Whitehouse, of the Royal Scottish Museum, Edinburgh, informed me that three pots from the Highsted cemetery had been offered to the museum as a gift. The donor was insistent that they should go to Edinburgh rather than Maidstone, but Miss Whitehouse kindly sent photographs and details of four pots, the fourth being retained by the donor. The pots are not necessarily some of those excavated in 1955, but three of them presumably come from the Belgic cemetery, the fourth coming from the adjacent late Roman cemetery originally reported in 1934.

1. Butt beaker, dark grey-brown ware; height 13.3 cm.; rim diameter 8.2cm. Registered no: of Royal Scottish museum 1978.373.

2. Small 'S' profile jar, with single cordon at base of neck; dark greyware; height 8.9cm. rim diam. 7cm.1978.375.

3. Globular beaker, with bead rim & groove above belly; red ware; height 8.9cm; rim 10.9cm. in private possession.

4. Flanged bowl, late Roman: grey-brown ware; hgt.6.9cm.; rim diam.16cm. 1978. 374.

So who was the mysterious thief? And why were all the notes stolen also? It points to the possibility he/she was an archaeologist ...... one would have hoped that when he/or she was 'laid back in the closet' that the truth would out, so far it has not.

I found the original 'East Kent Gazette' report available in Sittingbourne library. There were two articles, one on 12th August and one on 9th Sept. 1955. Here is the transcribed text of those, courtesy of the "East Kent Gazette":-

"ROMAN BURIAL GROUND UNEARTHED AT HIGHSTED"

"Fourteen skeletons found and more expected .

A full scale excavation is being carried out by Maidstone Museum and members of the Kent Archaeological Society in a chalk quarry at Highsted, where during the past few weeks 14 skeletons have been uncovered. They form part of a Roman burial ground dating back to between 75B.C. and 20A.D.

Officials of the Kent Archaeological Society and of Maidstone Museum have endeavoured for the last six weeks to keep the location of the site secret so that valuable evidence would not be destroyed by "amateur diggers". While excavation is being carried out they ask people not to hamper them by visiting the site until all the evidence has been gathered. For this reason the Gazette has not published anything about it until to-day.

The first find was made by Mr. Archie Pack, of Lower Murston, while he was excavating chalk for the Associated Portland Cement Manufacturers Ltd. As he drove his mechanical digger into the soft earth above the chalk face, a skull rolled down the bank. When he investigated the site he found other bones, and Mr. J. R. Rutherford, the A.P.C.M.'s manager at Murston, was informed.

Further finds were made by Mr. Frederick George Winter of 26, Murston Rd., Sittingbourne, who unearthed other skeletons and pieces of pottery.

Mr. D. T. A. Ponton, local secretary and a member of the K.A.S. and Miss M. Bloomstein, of Maidstone Museum are superintending the excavations. On Monday, with two other helpers, Mr. Ponton unearthed several skeletons, one which was found with two pieces of well preserved pottery against the skull. It is believed that one of the skeletons may be considerably older than the remainder which have been found. It was lying in earth which has become blackened. None of the other burial places have shown this characteristic.

Full extent of find not known

Mr.Ponton emphasised that the full extent of the find is not yet known. Bones found on the site will be sent to Guy's Hospital, London, where they will be examined by a pathologist to determine their exact age. Two distinct forms of pottery have been found which cover two different periods, and all the evidence will have to be gathered before a final assessment and report is made. It is expected that in the next few weeks more skeletons will be uncovered.

The site has in the past yielded other finds to archaeologists. About 1937 a lead coffin - now in Maidstone Museum-was uncovered, and various bones and implements have been discovered in the vicinity.

Among those working on the site this week was Mr. H. Berry, of 57 Woodstock Road, Sittingbourne, who is hoping soon to form a local group of the Faversham Soc. He told the Gazette that the area was rich in finds for historians and he felt that an organised local body should be formed. Faversham Historical Society were recruiting members from this area and later in the year it was hoped to form a local group.

Also helping on Tuesday were four young schoolboys - David Feakes and Martin Stevens, of Rodmersham, Hugh Allen, the son of Mr. D. Allen (Clerk to Sittingbourne and Milton Urban District Council) and Harry Hubbard".

Somehow I sympathise with the 'thief' if he held some sort of grudge against the diggers for their superior attitude. The words apostrophised so astutely by the reporter must have sounded so patronising. K.A.S. is an amateur group ……. is it just that some were deemed more amateur than others? Sadly, it seems to me from the static I have had, that this attitude that only the elite few can do a 'professional' job, still persists in some quarters. Perhaps I am too mundane, I have the view that everyone can be an archaeologist to a greater or lesser extent .

Observation is the initial key to being a good scientist and the same applies to the science/art of archaeology ….but I digress, there was a further entry in the paper on Sept. 9th. 1955 as follows :-

"QUARRY YIELDED 26 SKELETONS"

"Late discovery prolonged excavation work.

Discovery of yet another skeleton at the Highsted quarry burial ground at the week-end prolonged the work of excavation, which was due to finish on Sunday.

The total number of skeletons found during the excavation was 26, of which six had been cremated. The skeleton shown in our photograph is that of a six-foot man.

The fact that he was buried in a more elaborate grave some three feet below the turf level leads experts to think that he was a man of some importance. On various parts of the skeleton traces of burned wood were found. It is believed that these could have been left after the performance of some burial rite.

Another of the skeletons found within the last week is thought to be that of a child. It is only 46 inches high.

Earlier this week Mr. D. T. A. Ponton, who has been in charge of the excavation for the Kent Archaeological Society at the invitation of the A.P.C.M. Ltd. was completing his work of closing the site."

There are various points about the find that have not been mentioned in these reports that I can remember were said at the time. Although I was only 11, the scenario had such an impression on me that they are locked in my memory (hopefully accurately!)

One grave had several of the geode stones or 'sling shots' (mentioned in Chapter 5)

The six or so 'burnt' graves (see the 9th September entry) were not true cremations …but it was supposed at the time that they had been burnt for some 'ritual' reason. But how about a tragedy of a burning house one might ask?

But were there further clues? It seems the graves were within a rectangular ditched area and thrown in this ditch were older pots ……. this again gives the scenario of a rushed job and an Iron Age burial hastily dug: when the grave diggers came across older funerary urns did they place them in the surrounding ditch and re-bury everything?

This six feet long skeleton was found about three feet below turf level at Highsted Quarry. The remains are believed to be those of a "V.I.P." and were found with traces of burned wood probably used in a burial rite.

The site of the Roman burial ground has been sectioned off for excavation and is here being discussed by archaeologists.

Mr. D. T. A. Ponton (left) at the excavation. With him are Mr. J. R. Rutherford and Dr. R. G. Birch.

Lending a helping hand in clearing the site were Martin Stevens, Hugh Allen, David Feakes and Harry Hubbard.

These photographs are retaken from the East Kent Gazette in Sittingbourne Library. The original E. K. G. photos were destroyed in a flood. Thanks are due to the Library and E. K. Gazette for permission to reprint them here.

The graves were dated by a single La Tene III brooch. But look at the headline "Roman" graves. Why did the archaeologists say that ...when it is a pre-Roman date that they gave? All rather confusing I think, even aimed to confuse? Did they know something extraordinary about the graves that they were still holding back? Perhaps we shall never know ...it was so strange that Mr. Ponton and Mr. Berry died so shortly after as people said at the time ...like a Tutankhamen curse! But I do not believe in curses, but as Omar Khayyam in his poetry suggests ....it could be fate.

Here is a photograph not published in the paper that was taken by Arthur Page:- This grave distinctly shows a dark line of soil colour change that denotes a ditch.

My **guesses** and queries about the inconsistencies of the 1955 dig are these :-

The dating of the graves could be all cock-eyed because the La Tene brooch could very well have been an old one, a family heirloom passed down through a family, much as they are today. That would explain why they could be "Roman" in date as Mr. Ponton said and in fact as late as 40-60A.D.?

Were they all interred at the same time?

That seems likely, because of the surrounding ditch. The large funerary urns could be ones in-between that they did not disturb in digging the later date graves. "Two distinct forms of pottery have been found which cover two periods" the report said.

Was the 'more important' grave a chief?: he had a spear I think, I vaguely remember seeing it, but perhaps my memory over some forty five years plays tricks!

So were they warriors in a battle against the Romans? Did the chief get killed and most of his thanes? Was a funeral pyre hastily made in which case the bodies would not have burnt very well ...hence the semi-cremation? The number of women interred might suggest their leader was a woman.

Was the 'child' in fact a dwarf?; even in 1955 they would have been able to detect that! Chiefs sometimes had dwarf retainers. So where are the notes from Guys' Hospital? Were those stolen also?

The bones are now in Maidstone Museum. Surely it would be an excellent thesis for a research student currently at University.

I have only put forward a theory as to what happened .....I may be entirely wrong ..... but it makes a good story .....only waiting for someone more dedicated than I to research and get closer to the truth than I have done. What dismays me somewhat is the fact that all these people *(and they were people remember!)* are now ignominiously incarcerated in a museum forgotten about. They could be my ancestors and I can now entirely sympathise with the Indians of North America who object that the bones of so many Native American's are also in museum vaults. If they were your parents ....what would you feel then? But it is only parent's parent's times 80.

I will finish this chapter with a poem that Alison Hawkins wrote soon after the 1955 graves were found when she was scarcely ten:-

HIGHSTED 1955

The bones were yellow
The graves seemed shallow
Almost two thousand years old,
Uncovered when a skull rolled
In front of a bulldozer
To the surprise of the driver.
An ancient British burial place.
Once covered without a trace.
I stood and looked in wonderment
(They had been digging chalk for cement)
At the unfleshed bones
My first sight amongst the stones
Of anything human dead,
I was ten. My mother said
"It's of great historic interest".
But I thought "Let them rest".

Photos by Arthur Page

Note:
The shallowness of the graves was possibly because the mound of earth forming a barrow above them had long been flattened by the plough or deliberately removed.
David Perkins (Thanet Trust) has found that there are as many barrows in Thanet per acre as there are in Wiltshire. ...its just that they have been ploughed out! It is not illogical to surmise that there may be an equal density on mainland Kent

Chapter 3

Early Investigations, 1985-1995

I first knew of the possible settlement site in 1977 after I came back to Rodmersham from Canada in August of that year. Standing on the village Green on afternoons to meet my eldest daughter from school, I found myself talking to Alison Hawkins, reminiscing, (we went to Romersham school together) and our friendship went from there. She told me about the banks she had noticed that fitted the theory that the 'Iron Age people' lived there. She told me her mother could remember them planting the orchard in the 1930's. They cut the wood 'stumping it' and merely planting the young fruit trees without flattening any of the banks and ditches.

*Till now the doubtful dusk reveal'd
The knolls once more where, couch'd at ease
The white kine glimmer'd and the trees
Laid their dark arms about the field."
Tennyson*

Sometime in early 1985 the old cherry orchard was grubbed out in the field below the site. It was then that I contacted Garth Doubleday, the owner, and told him of the I.A. settlement possibilty. He was very interested and he, myself, and my brother David walked the site together.

Now, some archaeologists maintain that sites are 'safe' under orchards, but when 50 year old cherries are knocked over the soil is torn back to the sub-soil.

Here is a recent picture, note the red clay of the sub-soil. If it is then deep ploughed so much of the archaeology gets mangled in the top soil. **In fact most of the prehistoric archaeology is in the top soil.** Only pits beneath the plough line tend to survive. Despite what the archaeologists may tell you and what people tend to believe, the East Kent countryside has much of its ancient archaeology immediately under the turf: no feet of black soil covering it as in urban areas! You will see what I mean in the photographs of our investigations (chapter 6).

Grubbed Cherry Orchard

George Payne, last century, describes a Roman site near Blacklands, Teynham, with the pavement visible on the surface! How this comes about is that the soil tends to slide down hill as it is ploughed then eroded by the weather. Sites towards the top of a ridge have largely disappeared over a span of 2000 years. So despite what some archaeologists fear, metal detectorists help not hinder <u>**so long as they report what they find,**</u> and they are becoming invaluable in informing archaeologists of the position of previously unknown sites.

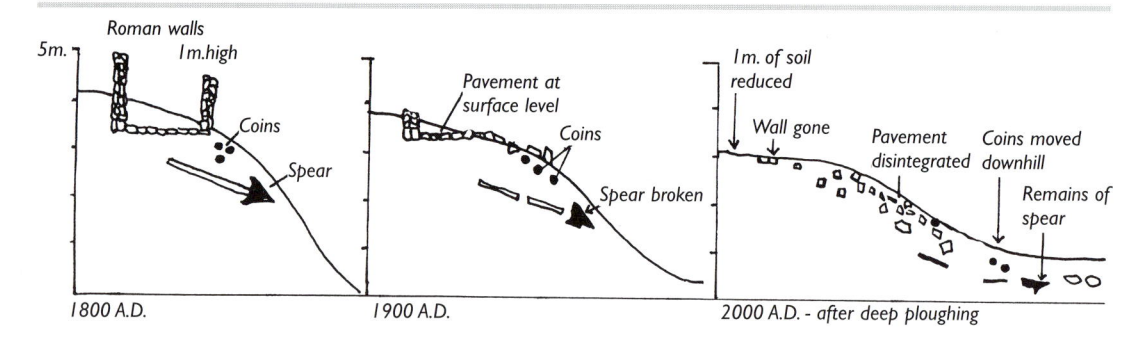

1800 A.D. — Roman walls 1m.high, Coins, Spear

1900 A.D. — Pavement at surface level, Coins, Spear broken

2000 A.D. - after deep ploughing — 1m. of soil reduced, Wall gone, Pavement disintegrated, Coins moved downhill, Remains of spear

Here is a diagram to help explain what I have just said:-

We have had several very reliable metal detectorists trawl the whole site but few metal objects have shown up ..... mostly pieces of iron, and just one bronze eyelet ring ....no coins unfortunately!

Open ground and scope for field walking was limited. The fruit trees were only cultivated around their trunks, the woodland was covered in leaf litter and brambles and the slope towards the quarry was always under grass.

Moles came to the rescue!

One of the first sherds of prehistoric pottery was found by 11 year old Elinor in 1985 after the suggestion we scattered the soil on each mole hill and looked carefully for items.

Her sharp eyes spotted a piece of Bronze Age/Iron Age transition pottery.

But our luck in finding many other pieces of pottery at this stage seemed remote. It was not until an archaeologist from Canterbury Archaeological Trust came to our rescue and showed us what to look for, (ancient pottery rarely 'shouts out' and often is very dark matching the soil), that we found more numerous Iron Age sherds mostly in the vicinity of the bank and inside ditch.

Bronze Age sherd from the mole hill

However, we did find this piece of iron that was of remarkable quality but somehow, did not appear to be modern. It has been suggested that it is an Iron Age ingot.

Bronze ring from the area of the ditch

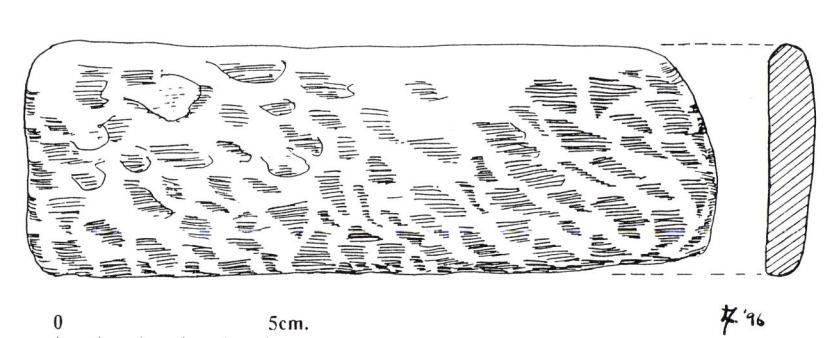

Linking with this piece of iron and tending to confirm that it is Iron Age are these numerous pieces of Romano-British iron slag. It is difficult to say whether they were pre-Roman or produced in Roman times. The largest piece came from the lower field near the farm house, but the smaller pieces, showing the characteristic 'flow' of bloomery slag, came from a ploughed field nearer the wood. (Orchard grubbed around 1993). Although Romano-British iron slag is common in Sussex it is much rarer in this part of Kent.

Tribute to our friendly mole!

Quite a few worked flints were collected in these early forays also. In fact the whole site seems to be strewn with Neolithic and earlier Mesolithic flints.

Iron slag from Highsted Farm discovered when two of the orchards were ploughed.

One particular type common on site seemed to be a blade in which the 'handle' area had its cortex (outside rough skin of the flint) left on. Perhaps this was devised to help in hafting. ...the rough area (like a galvanised nail) might grip the wood of the haft better. I found one of these also in a bank in Cheyney Wood, the other side of the valley.

Early in the 1990's the square orchard area was grubbed out and when the bulldozers levelled it the inside ditch was sadly lost. I had a very bad leg

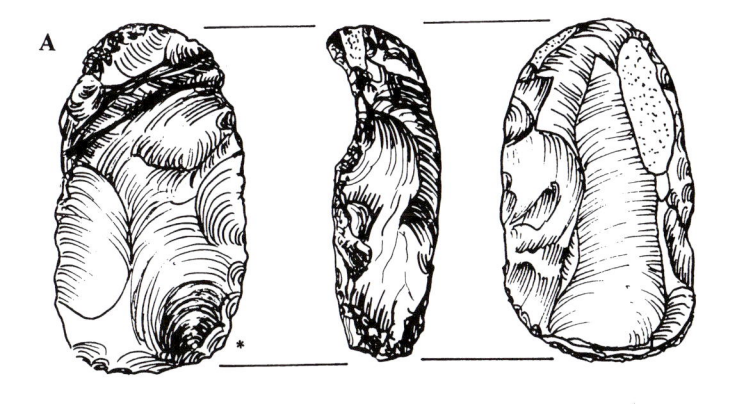

A Hooked tool (Neolithic) with definite worked artificially cut groove. Areas of the tool also indicate use as a striking tool. * Note the distinct conchoidal fracture (looks like a shell)
B Worked flake (Mesolithic/Neolithic)
C Knife blade, (broken) with distinctive area of cortex (probably left on to enhance adhesion to a wooden shaft).
D Microlith - Mesolithic blade (broken).

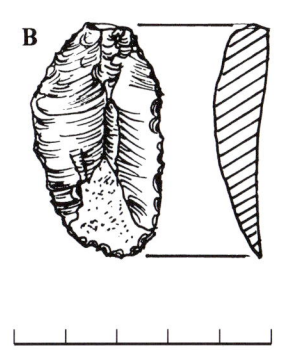

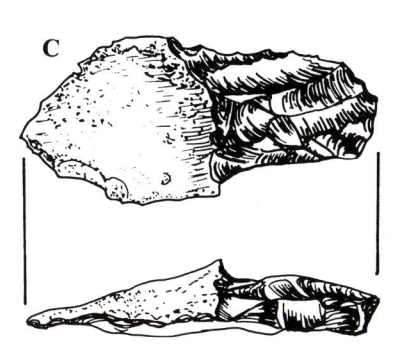

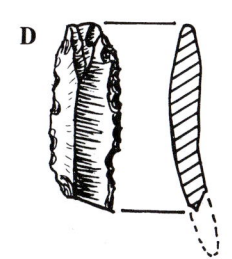

More worked flints

Blade (found 24.4.94)
possibly Mesolithic

7.5 cm

9.5 cm

Darker centre

Mesolithic core
of brown flint
11 facets

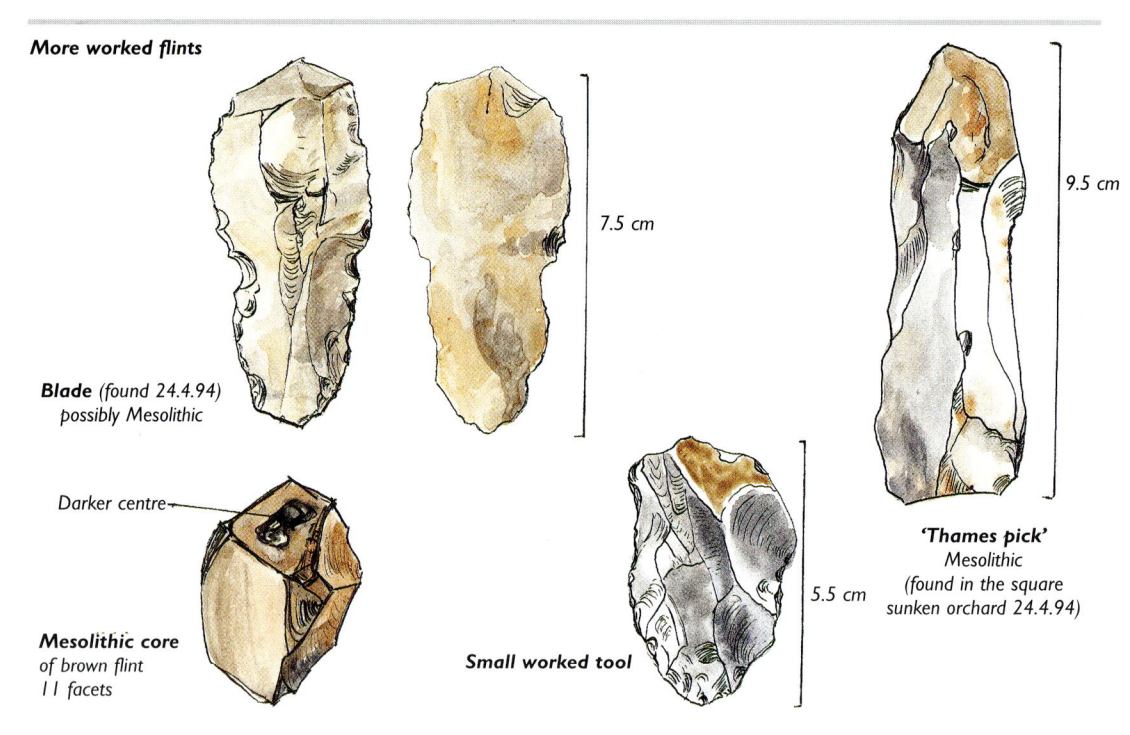

Small worked tool

5.5 cm

'Thames pick'
Mesolithic
(found in the square
sunken orchard 24.4.94)

A few examples of the Worked Flints.
These were found in the northern square orchard area of the site. Most are Mesolithic, some Neolithic.

fracture during this time and was unable to keep an eye on things. You will see in the 1985 picture that ditch is quite distinct. When we later had a geophysical survey done it did not show at all and all that the print out showed was how thoroughly it had been obliterated! Still, that is how farming goes these days ...to make a living in fruit growing, old cherry trees have to be grubbed out and smaller trees, more productive and easier to pick, replace them.

N ↑ grid north

Ditch on the inside of the main bank in November 1985 when it was clearly visible. Now, unfortunately, this feature has been lost. Beena Patel, on the left, helped search for it in the 1996 dig. Elinor Hawkins, on the right, found the B.A. sherd.

24

In 1992 a member of Canterbury Archaeological Trust (C.A.T). walked the site with us and showed us what to look for regarding pieces of pottery (sherds as they are called in archaeology). We realised what we had missed! Along the top of the bank beside the now missing ditch, were several pieces of Belgic grog ware. This is the term for a certain type of Iron Age ware found in Kent that was manufactured in late Iron Age through to the Roman occupation. To strengthen the clay body of the pot and to help dissipate heat during cooking (i.e. so the pots do not crack) people discovered that to crush up broken pots and knead the fine pieces back into the new clay worked very well. Often flint is heated in a fire till it is brittle then pulverised and added to the clay. Pulverised flint is still a constituent of pottery clay and glazes today.

These Belgic pots do not have very much flint inclusion but they do have a lot of grog.

'Belgic' grog ware sherds from the bank/ditch area. Note:- it is easy to record them like this on the scanner.

During different ages people got accustomed to using different clay fills and it is by looking very carefully with a hand lens or microscope that one can become proficient in identifying the different pots. However, it is not so simple! Flint tempered ware was common in the Bronze Age, but it is also found in other ages such as Medieval times! The outside finish of the pot and the style also changes within different Ages. Sometimes individual potters made a 'one off' pot much as they do today so unless the pot is found in the same layer (context) as other items it is sometimes difficult to say what it is! But on the whole the identification of sherds has got to such a fine art that a whole site can sometimes be positively dated by just one piece of very typical pot.

The Bronze Age Dover boat, found by C.A.T. in 1992, had just one sherd found beneath it. From this sherd it was possible to date the whole find, which was later confirmed by the dating of the timber itself.

Getting back to our few sherds on the bank. Normally if sherds are found in the top soil it is not acceptable to say "Oh, here is an Iron Age site" or whatever. The reason being that the sherds could have strayed, being spread upon the field with dung from a farmstead. Or someone may have taken 'lunch' to work in the fields then dropped the pot! But either argument would more or less accept that there was an Iron Age farmstead in the vicinity.

However, the top soil finds here on Highsted Farm were a little different from a single 'chance' find.

1. We had photographic and farm proof of a rectangular enclosure with an inside ditch and that ditch seems to have been a repository for a variety of pots of different ages.

Hollow way looking west in 1985.

2. The 26 Iron Age graves found in 1955 were only 200 metres or less away.

3. The banks were very marked in places, definitely man made, height in the wood some 15 metres, with a deep encircling "hollow way"

4. The presence of so many pieces of iron slag.

5. A considerable selection of worked flints.

6. A Late Bronze Age loop and socket axe was found 200 metres to the west in 1927.

So the overall proof that we had found a settlement site covering several different eras was rising.

But the main proof of the site still lay in its banking system. This was complicated to work out and some of the banks had been lost particularly on the eastern side. The 'hollow way' was the most impressive feature and I was sure that the archaeologist who had viewed the site for the owner, Garth

Looking east up the main bank from the Boundary Stone.
Bank at this point is some 20 metres high.
Year 2000.

Tile fragments found west of the farmhouse. Thickness of the largest piece, colour and inclusions in the others suggests they are Roman and not medieval or modern.

Doubleday, had not bothered to walk up into the wood. (see chapter 5) It is very difficult to photograph a bank to give the full scope of its size. Last year, 2000, with recent coppicing it was easier to see it again.

In the early days we had walked most of the site but the lack of open ploughed soil areas was restricted. However, the young cherry orchard to the east of the banks, closer to the Highsted Farm house, had quite a lot of tile fragments. Some of these appear to be Roman. So if there was a Roman Villa/farm that is where it would likely be. On an aerial photograph taken in 1951 there is a vague lighter rectangle in this orchard that could indicate a building.

Interestingly this is exactly one Roman mile from Pitstock Farm that shows evidence of a Roman building (aerial evidence/tile/amphora) and this again is one Roman mile from Little Newbury Roman Villa (excavated by B. Philp in 1985).

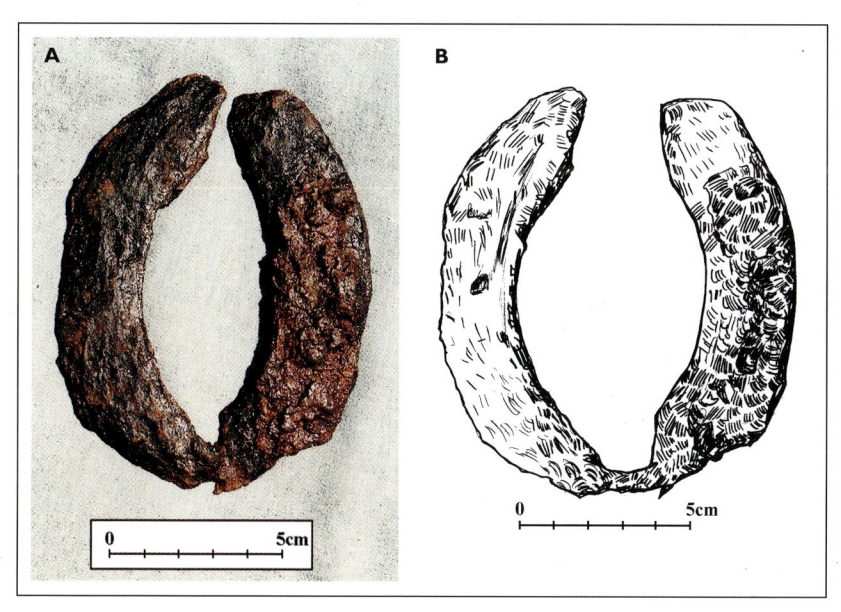

A. *"Iron Age" Horseshoe from the north bank found 5 metres from the ancient cannon bone (see chapter 5). This horseshoe has now been included because it is possibly Iron Age and of importance. It was found in 1986 and many people scoffed that it could not be dated! But luck was eventually in! For in 2000, I found a drawing of an Iron Age horseshoe in "Belgic Britons" by Gordon Ward that is remarkably similar! All one can say for sure is that the horse that threw this shoe had worn it down at the toe as if it had done some considerable galloping!*

B. *Drawing of the shoe with the worn toe straightened out.*

Ancient trackway in the Doddington valley, part of "Old Street".

Chapter 4

Trackways and Waterways.

Quoting the Bible yet again ...but it is a record of Bronze Age/Iron Age people and the Galatians were Celts! I am almost certain that British Celts were their dyslexic cousins. Ninevites were said to be an entire city of people that *"could not tell their right hand from their left"*....classic dyslexia! I spent several years learning, when I was a kid, which was my right hand and which my left!

Dyslexic people often have an enormously developed right temporal lobe of the brain with a good spatial awareness, knowledge and grasp of geometry and trigonometry, can draw well, but ....they hate writing things down!

To try and say that ancient Britons 'did not have extensive trackways' or 'could not site lines' or 'did not make the most direct routes' to me are invalid statements. Not nearly enough research has been done into ancient trackways, **especially in Kent.** Ancient Celts did their 'writing' on the landscape, follow my arguments to the end of the book and you will see that that is true.....

It is well known that Watling Street 'was made by the Romans'. A straight road from Sandwich to London and beyond ....but it is less well known that there was a road called 'Old Street' running roughly parallel, crossing the River Medway at Cuxton (not Rochester) and going on towards 'London' as it is now. There must have been Celtic roads: how else do you suppose the Celts had their chariots lined up on Dover's Cliffs to meet Caesar in 54B.C.? My 'Trackway Map' of road systems in this part of Kent will help to explain the situation, as I think it was. Oad St. and Hole St. are on line to equal an 'Old' Street.

Many Roman roads had been worked out and recorded by Ivan Margary in his excellent book, *"Roman Roads in Britain"*, but then people tend to sit back and think his work is a Bible and that is all there were!

*What then are all the "streets" of Kent? Many are so straight. Which of these trackways are actually made by the Romans and which are improved Celtic routes? A difficult question to answer. But it is unlikely that the numerous 'streets' were originally *'Saxon drove ways'* as some people believe! The Saxons moved in on a very well established Iron Age, then Roman managed, field/farming/industrial system with the roads already in place. The routes connecting Woodstock with this grid system are evident: let me try and explain using the **Trackway Map** as a reference.

Stand at the crossroads and look; ask for the ancient path , ask where the good way is and walk in it , ..."
Jeremiah 6 v.16 N.I.V

*Some people reading this might be thinking "Of course there were ancient trackways in Kent", but when I was about to ask an influential Kent archaeologist of his opinion on Bronze Age alignments and possible trackways I made the mistake of using the term 'ley': he then threw out the comment "Oh we do not believe in 'ley lines' and little green men!" I was so stunned by the sarcasm I kept quiet ....till now. Perhaps similar scoffing is why Kent's trackways have never been truly determined. Since then, when I was so squashed flat, long lines of B.A. posts have been found near Monkton, Thanet .....scoffing tends to delay discoveries and knowledge ....just as the flat-Earth policy did!

Wychling Church in its woodland setting.

Roman flue tile, Wychling Wood.

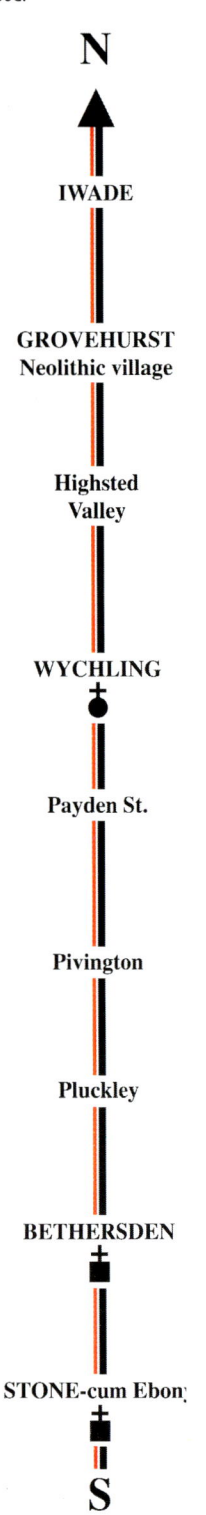

N ↑

IWADE

GROVEHURST
Neolithic village

Highsted Valley

WYCHLING

Payden St.

Pivington

Pluckley

BETHERSDEN

STONE-cum Ebony

S

Wychling Waymarks*
TQ9125.5488.

The straight Half Mile Path is most likely Neolithic or Bronze Age. It is dead straight; so much so that one can see right down the footpath from one end to the other. On days that I was late for school, it was quicker to cycle down it (rather than the road) but I hated doing so because the slightest wobble and one was thrown into the fence on either side. The alignment of the track is magnetic north, set at a time it coincided with todays position ....5° west of grid north?

The straight line heads for Wychling Church and George Payne, the local archaeologist of the last century, remarked on this and also (like myself) thought the track was ancient. Wychling has a medieval church ...but its village reputedly died in the plague ....but is it just medieval? No one has looked! The mysterious woods have lumps and bumps ...I walked them recently ....did not find anything medieval, but I found some very distinctive Roman flue tile with a roller printed pattern! So if the Romans were there .....who else was? It is a superb vantage point! Besides the Roman tile there are/were in the vicinity, ancient stones set at special points. From the 1909 Map it seems clear the position of these sarsens was once significant. These piled near Wychling* have been moved. I can find very few in the positions logged by the Victorians on the map ....which were presumably their original waymark places.

If the projection of the Wychling line is carried further, through a point on the Downs, it eventually sites on Stone-cum-Ebony: and in that church is an ancient Mithraic altar stone. Where it was exactly, before the church was built, is not known. The bulls around it are very indistinct, I have outlined to make them clearer.

The fact that the older Kent churches are mostly if not all, on far, far older sites, is an important one, especially in my argument that they are on ancient co-ordinates. Here is an example on one on a mound or tun.

Mithraic Altar Stone in Stone-cum-Ebony church.

NEWINGTON CHURCH :-

'New' in the case of Newington probably means built close to an older Roman site (ref. Wallenberg) and only 0.5 miles away considerable Roman finds occurred at Keycol Hill; and where did Romans so often build? ....on older Celtic sites ...and they honoured 'sacred' sites of conquered people. It appears that the Saxons and Normans did too, for both Wychling and Boxley have ancient sarsen stones set in the foundations. If other Kent churches do also, it becomes a project for someone to follow up!

Boxley has one on the N.W. and the S.W. corners. Wychling's is on the S.E. corner. One of the most convincing local sarsens is one under Newnham church wall.

So far I have only shown a North → South line ...the East → West of "Old Street" looks a bit wobbly I hear someone say, and its not due East → West! No, it is not, but let's look at it first.

"Old Street" is likely a corruption of Hole Street and in broad Kentish, Oad, would be pronounced "O-oo-w-d"street: the vowels are extended dipthongs and 'l's become 'w's, with ending consonants very soft. Kentish people were notorious in dropping 'h's like the Cockneys, and they also added them when they were not there!

*It has been suggested by some that these are "unimportant" stones dragged off the fields by the farmers. BUT they are as big as the 'Merry Maidens' in Cornwall & Kent's megalithic sites have been so poorly recorded and so many destroyed! See chap.14

Wardwell Wood

NEWINGTON 9·11·00

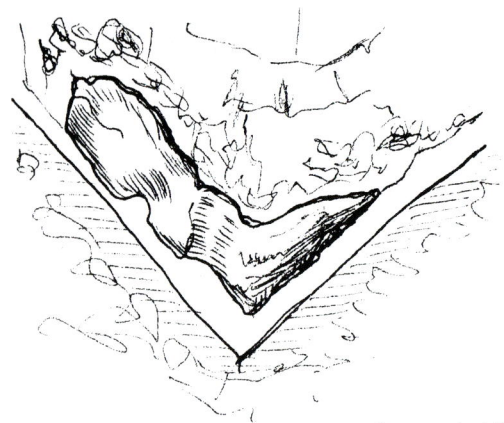

Sarsen under N.W. corner of Boxley Church.

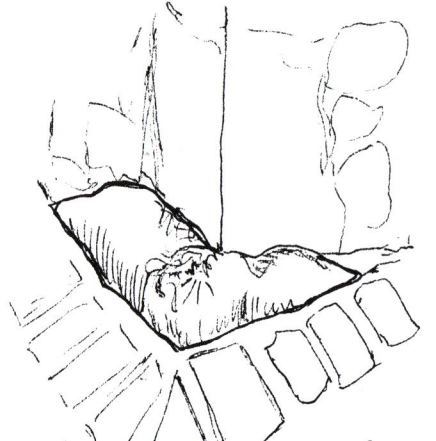

Sarsen under S.W. corner of Boxley Church.

WYCHLING
Roman tile set in the East Wall. →

← Sarsen under S.E. corner.
Note also the modern bench mark.

Wychling - from the S.W. - note the blue line on the horizon is the sea at Whitstable. It only needs a clearing in the wood (a "LEY") to see that far.

So Hole could become "O-oo-w-l" street and old can become Hole! **But,** perhaps it is that way around! Perhaps the method of siting used was a system of very large wooden poles stood in holes. They would then have to be wedged with flints probably a great pile of them. The flints would have long been robbed out to metal the numerous lanes...leaving holes ....but most now filled in. Bronze Age sites invariably have lines of post holes.

Sorry, I am starting to mix facts with theory! Let's get back to a visual fact. Look at the Trackway Map and use a ruler and line Stone, near Faversham, with West Malling. Notice all the churches and sarsens on that line? It is a line marked also with very closely adjacent

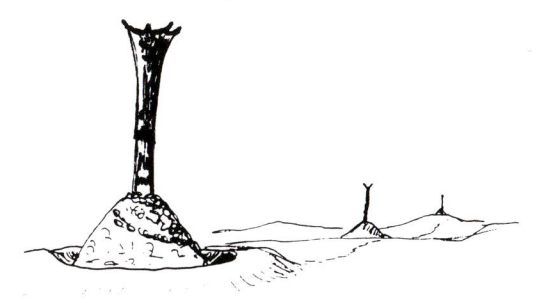

Waymarks still in place at Westfield Wood, Blue Bell Hill.

33

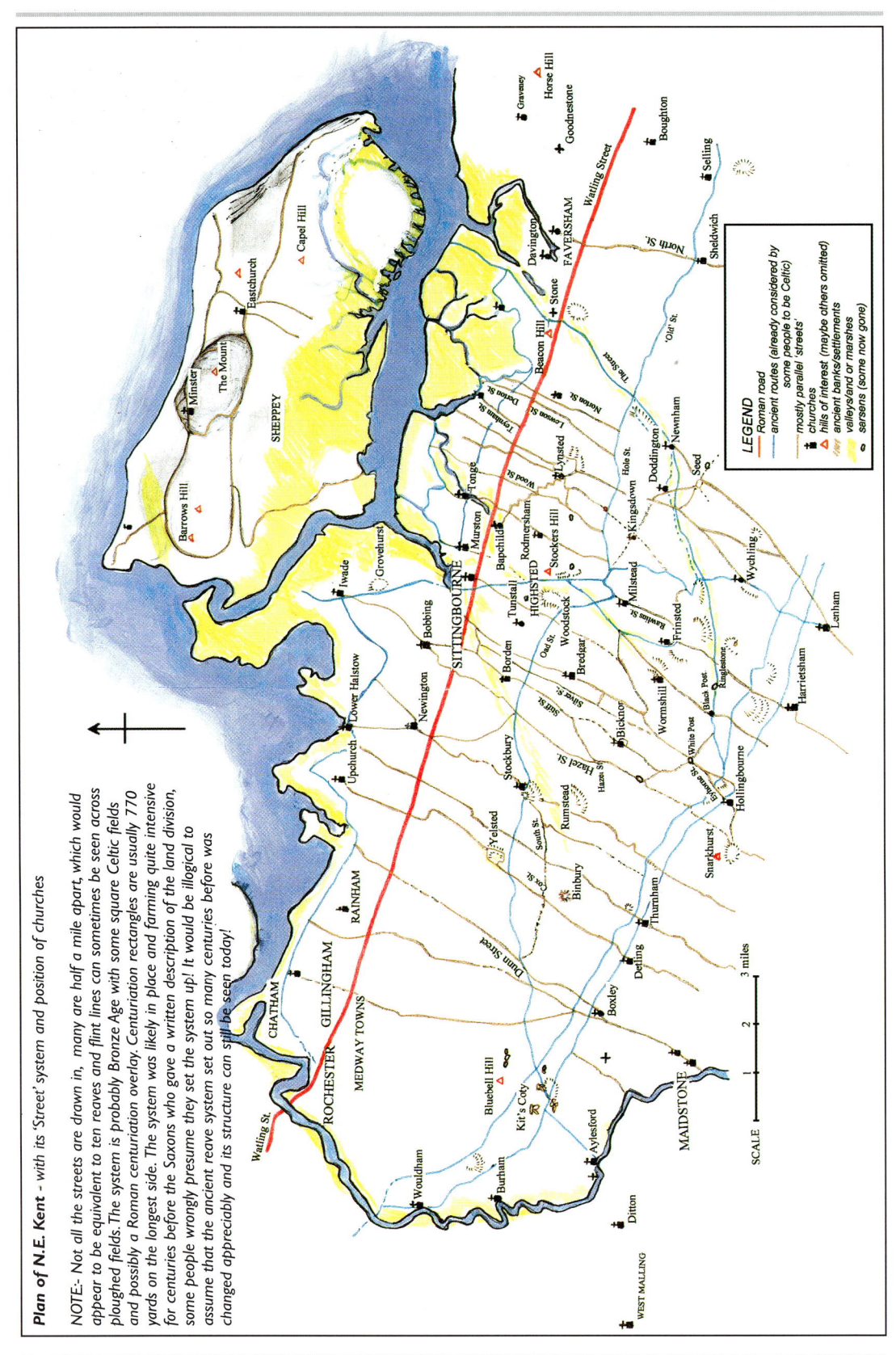

Plan of N.E. Kent - with its 'Street' system and position of churches

NOTE:- Not all the streets are drawn in, many are half a mile apart, which would appear to be equivalent to ten reaves and flint lines can sometimes be seen across ploughed fields. The system is probably Bronze Age with some square Celtic fields and possibly a Roman centuriation overlay. Centuriation rectangles are usually 770 yards on the longest side. The system was likely in place and farming quite intensive for centuries before the Saxons who gave a written description of the land division, some people wrongly presume they set the system up! It would be illogical to assume that the ancient reave system set out so many centuries before was changed appreciably and its structure can still be seen today!

hill points (look back at my picture of Newington, it has a second hill or "tun" just to the north = Wardwell Wood).

One can amuse oneself in tracing this East → West hill and church line miles across country ...even to Stonehenge ...... and beyond. Is it an illusion, an imaginary line, not a fact at all? Many people think the majority of Kent's churches are 'manorial', i.e. built where the Lord of the Manor dictated ....but most that I seem to have looked at do not appear to be determined by a manor ....exception Frinsted? But very recent metal detector finds indicate a Roman site very near to that church.

Notice that this 'church line' is exactly at right angles to the Wychling line. Note also at this point 'lane ' in Kentish is pronounced "Lie-ee-ne".

So, there is an East-West Lane, whether you accept it or not. No doubt those with left hemisphere dominated minds will start quibbling at this point, if they have not been doing so all along! Unwritten and undrawn lines on the landscape they will reject as 'unfactual', but people versed in "ley-lines" will wonder why I am trying to prove a point that they already accept! But for the doubters, here are further, more solid, facts:-

Diagonal lines :-The SW → NE roads are obvious and most have a 'street' name. Some of these can be traced right across to the Weald of Kent. Fact also, they invariably have a church at either end and one in the middle. I have not drawn all the SW lines else the map might become too confusing, neither have I drawn all the cross linking wiggly ones that could sometimes be Saxon additions. So now we have a compass but without the NW → SE co-ordinates.

It is fact that a right-handed person (using their left cerebal hemisphere) finds that direction more difficult to draw on a plan than NE → SW. But to a left handed person it is easy. It is possible that the NW → SE was considered more 'mystical' or the direction one rarely travelled! Perhaps a population with a high proportion of dyslexia (not wanting to write things down but very spatially aware) drew that direction in their minds and calculated it from landmarks. If you take a ruler, orientate it in NW → SE direction and slide it across the map, you will find that many of the churches line up as if they were on old marker points that can show the way. Fact is that one of the NW directions, that from Lynsted church, has a very tortuous zigzag track, maybe it is around field systems, but on the other hand.... it could be avoiding that "unwanted" direction! Locals call that road the 'Forty Corners.'

"Do not move your neighbours boundary stone... established long ago in the land that the Lord your God is giving you ." Deuteronomy 19.v.14.

Pity no one listened, we might have several stone circles left on Bluebell Hill and Eastling if they had! And more waymark stones still in position might help me to prove my theories!

Remember there was a strong megalithic culture in Kent and only the more spectacular sites have been retained so all the surface sarsens of the area would likely have been Neolithic 'significant' places 5000 years ago. George Payne writes around the turn of the 20th century that he regretted government policy that allowed the Royal Engineers to blow many of them up in demolition practice! Higsted Wood is littered with small pieces of sarsen as though split from a much larger stone.

But there is another place to look to prove the land sections and tracks in Kent are prehistoric. In Devon the landscape has been less tampered with and is closer to the Bronze Age condition. Oliver Rackham, in his marvellous book *"The Illustrated History of the Countryside"* p.72-75, describes the 'reaves' that traverse the landscape in a roughly N.E. → S.W. direction. They are a grid of parallel stony banks that delineate the Bronze Age field systems and are

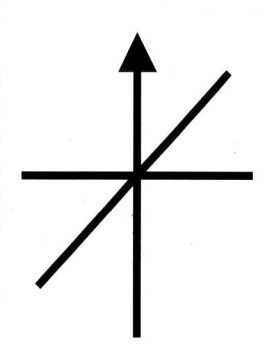

Devon reaves - reprinted from "The History of the Countryside" by kind permission of the author Oliver Rackham, and the publishers J.M. Dent & Sons.

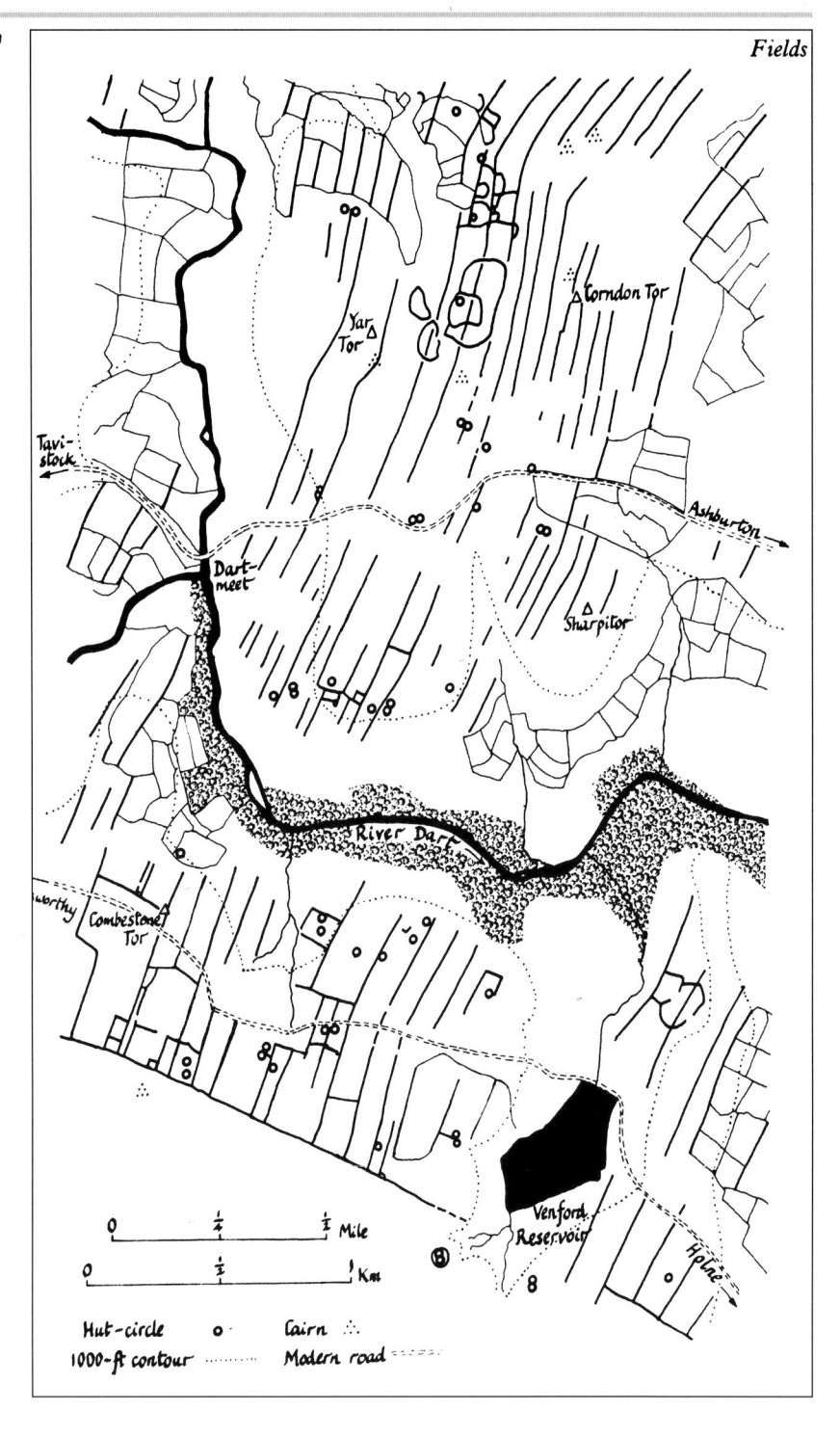

Fields

Hut-circle   o Cairn
1000-ft contour .... Modern road =====

typically 100 yards apart. He also describes them in his earlier book "The History of the Countryside" and I have reproduced that diagram here with his kind permission and the publishers J. M. Dent & Sons.

In his words he says "Reaves tell a story of country planning on a gigantic scale - of an organisation able to parcel out tens of square miles as it pleased, whose writ ran in the heights of Dartmoor, and which sets its rules of geometry above the practicalities of dealing with gorges and bogs. England has known nothing like this in the last 1,500 years. For a modern parallel we have to go to the land-allotments of Minnesota or Michigan."

In Kent the line of the parallel 'streets' closely resembles the Devon plan and there appear to have been approximately ten reaves between the streets (where streets are half a mile apart). The possibility they were in fact there is backed up by findings on Highsted Farm with a line of flint nodules in the bank and across the valley on Oak Tree Farm. Another flint line is visible on a field near Rawlings Street just south of Highsted. Now I have mentioned the possibility perhaps farmers will contribute more evidence of lines of flints they have encountered.

The line of these reaves both in Kent and in Devon appears to be (as I have said) on the SW → NE axis relative to magnetic north .....but there maybe another explanation for this alignment ......magnetic north varies as the 'bar magnet' within the Earth appears to wobble. Did it wobble far more at a distant point in the past? If it was as much as 20° east of grid north it is not possible that the reaves were set on magnetic north as it was at that time? I admit my knowledge of geophysics is not very good but now I have raised the possibility perhaps experts can calculate if this were possible? Chapter 11 considers this and other alignments in more detail.

Waterways

This chapter is also about waterways and so far I have only mentioned roads! Once someone tried to tell me the roads were designed like that *'because they followed the valleys'*! But they do not, and Oliver Rackham's words confirm what I had observed ....the valleys are largely independent from the road designs. The only concession is that there is usually a trackway along the rim of each valley and one just below the ridge, but still on high ground. *"You take the high road and I'll take the low road"* ....one does get to Scotland quicker if the town one is going to is in the valley! But the Celts were not quite as fool-hardy as us: in a climate much wetter and with a higher water table (from more

Bunces Farm, Tonge.

persistent rain) they probably did not live in the valley floor but only farmed the fertile soil. Settlements appear to be mostly on the southern hills of the valleys ...with banks facing down the valley and perhaps with woods as a defensive freize-de-chevaux to the north? Look along the scarp of the Downs, from Blue Bell Hill to Charing for more such sites.

Access to the sea was VERY important. This was a seafaring nation, not only farming the corn to feed Caesar's armies but shipping it across the Channel also.

Evidence of the harbours and ships is still to be excavated and found in the levels of Teynham, Luddenham, Conyer and Oare. But there is no doubt in my mind that it is there!

At various times the sea level has been different. It has been estimated by some archaeologists that it was "IN", in Roman times. That means Teynham Street was on the sea, Key street was probably a host of quays, (if it was not just the name of a pub) and Oare was probably a port for ore shipment.

The Highsted River and the 'Syndale' River ...or was it the Ludd, have long sunk beneath their gravel beds. Both valleys had gravel extracted in the 19th century and both have waterworks that are still avidly pumping the underground river water.

The Highsted River could have been navigatable as far as Highsted Farm on a rather muddy tidal estuary. Tonge was likely on the sea shore as the photograph of Bunces Farm indicates by the flat land surrounding the farm 'island'.

Tonge pond ran dry a few years ago as the water table of the Highsted Valley got so low ...no danger of that now!

Tonge castle ....is reputedly an old motte and bailey. From George Payne's description (and John Guy in *"Kent Castles"*) I would have guessed Neolithic! There are still sarsens hidden around in the area if you look carefully. **But how**

Looking across Tonge Pond to what remains of the castle.

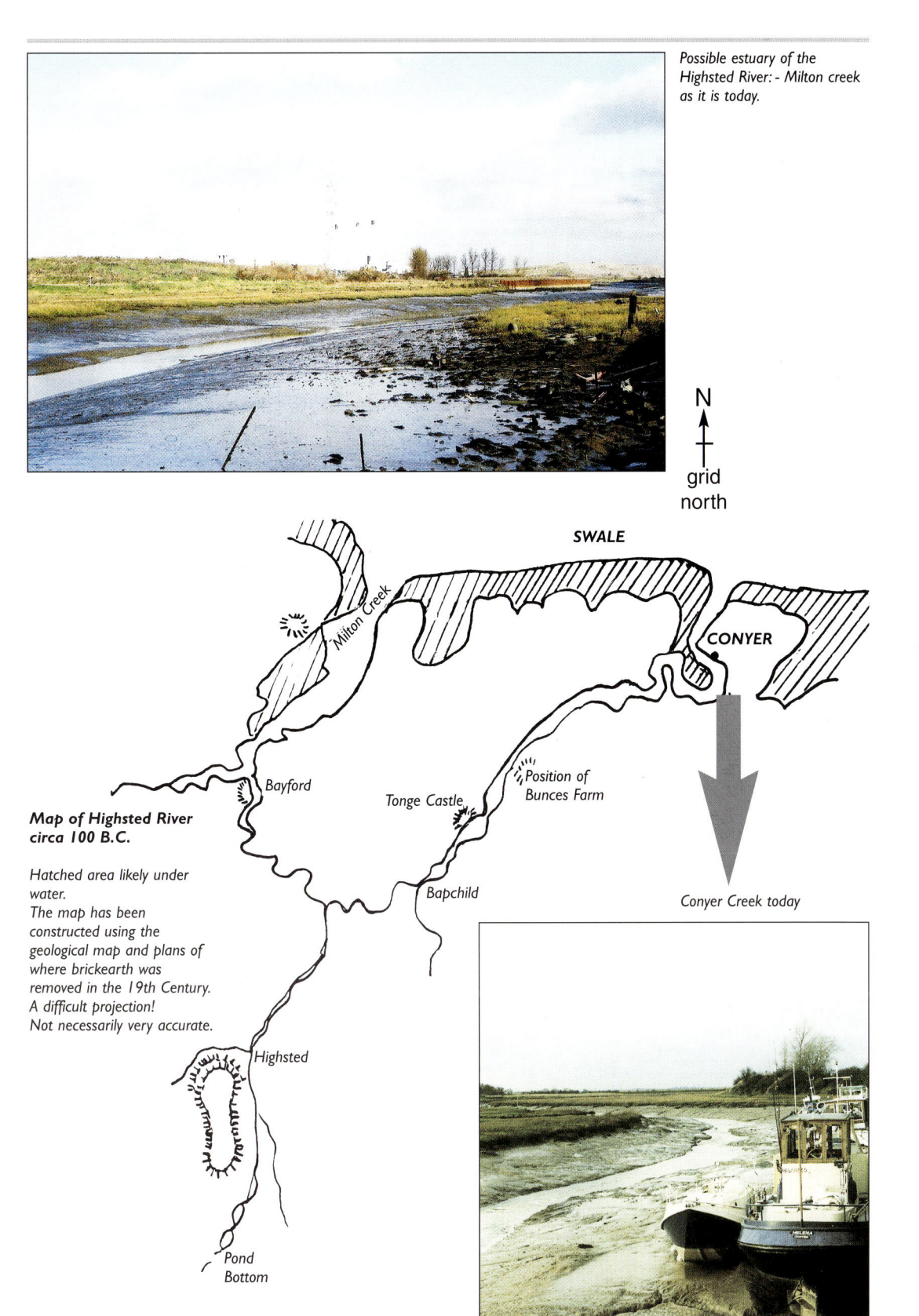

Possible estuary of the Highsted River: - Milton creek as it is today.

SWALE

CONYER

Milton Creek

Bayford

Tonge Castle

Position of Bunces Farm

Bapchild

Highsted

Pond Bottom

Conyer Creek today

Map of Highsted River circa 100 B.C.

Hatched area likely under water.
The map has been constructed using the geological map and plans of where brickearth was removed in the 19th Century.
A difficult projection!
Not necessarily very accurate.

did the Council allow a modern bungalow to be built right on the Castle mound? There was some archaeological investigation done but one wonders if it was sufficient? Modern sectioning of the moat behind the bungalow would be an interesting project.

Evidence that the Highsted River has not long been 'gone', in geological time, is in the name for the area higher up the valley. Locals have always called it Pond Bottom and on older maps 'Long Bottom', that would imply that there was, not so long ago, a chain of ponds in the bottom, remnants of that forgotten river. Water is very important and the Highsted River doubtless had a tributary stream flowing down from Woodstock ......hence my reconstruction drawings ...the site was almost surrounded by water.

Water supply:

Even though there was likely a Highsted River and a tributary flowing down the Woodstock valley to join it, that may not have been the drinking water supply. Remember, they were sophisticated and intelligent people not unlike ourselves, so would you like to drink where the sheep do? No, I feel that it is far more likely that they sank a well or wells. Most places in this part of Kent yield superior drinking water from the chalk. Many hill farmhouses of all centuries had a well, sometimes very deep ones, over 70 metres. One hollow in the orchard at Highsted the farm manager tells me will never fill, the earth always sinks again ....so presumably, it could be ... a well?

Water is the key to life and all life processes, both in real and 'spiritual' terms.

Life began in water.... and as you will see in Chapter 10, the electro-magnetism attached to it can appear rather strange ...but explicable.

Dowsing with a hazel switch - an age old method of finding water.

Chapter 5

"Wool over One's Eyes"

Knowledge should be open and available to all and to the benefit of all for education to grow and prosper. Now, with the modern internet, that ideal is becoming a reality. Granted the internet has drawbacks but I am not going into those here, but can only say that I hope archaeology will become more open in its approach to <u>everyone</u>. I welcome the day when we can all access the Sites and Monuments Record. If some people think this is a 'risk' and opens the way to 'unethical' people searching with metal detectors then legislation needs tightening and certain people educating. But one thing I am certain of, there cannot be different rules of access to information depending on 'who you are'!

> "He thought he saw a bank of sand
> With nought but rocks and ferns
> He looked again and found it was
> A pile of Belgic urns!"
> —— with apologies to Lewis Carroll

Our own opinions are often taken from our own experiences and this chapter is written with a good deal of humour ....if I couldn't laugh at some of the things that have happened and been said, I would have given up doing any archaeology years ago!

Negative people seem to abound in Kent, it is as if they are in their own "time warp", having a tradition to "put people off" and retain "a mystique" surrounding archaeology, a "culture of secrecy!" Am I exaggerating? Have a read of this chapter and form your own opinions! I have received a few apologies along the way for some of the comments said to me and I hope volunteer archaeologists will be <u>encouraged</u> in future to investigate unknown sites.

In 1985 after we had walked the site with the owner Garth Doubleday, it was obvious he was very interested and helpful and he said he would approach a Kentish Archaeologist for advice. Garth had been very intrigued by the graves found in 1955 in the chalk pit and had a similar interest as my brother and I.

But the answer came back from the archaeologist:-*"The banks were just plough banks!"* Now this could have been a genuine mistake, but Len Jay an archaeologist from Thanet (now sadly deceased) told us:-" *I am sure he is wrong! It **is** an Iron Age site and I would like you to prove it!"*

The mistake can be explained hopefully with the help of diagrams. Plough banks can form but the presence of a markedly square corner and an inside ditch should have alerted him to the fact there was more to the site.

Much later the same archaeologist was giving a talk at Dover, he showed a banking system found in North Kent that was Iron Age. After the talk I went up to him and asked if he remembered walking a site on Highsted Farm. He did. So then I asked tentatively whether he had ever walked up into Highsted

HIGHSTED BANKS

Diagram to explain the formation of PLOUGH BANKS

Non-typical inside ditch as at Highsted

Situation some 100 years ago

Woodland bank

Headland - for turning the plough

Movement of soil

Continued ploughing will increase the size of the bank and the soil will continue to creep down the slope

Bank larger

Trackway

Second bank forming

Soil still reducing and moving down hill

At Present Time

Positive lynchet (not present at Highsted)

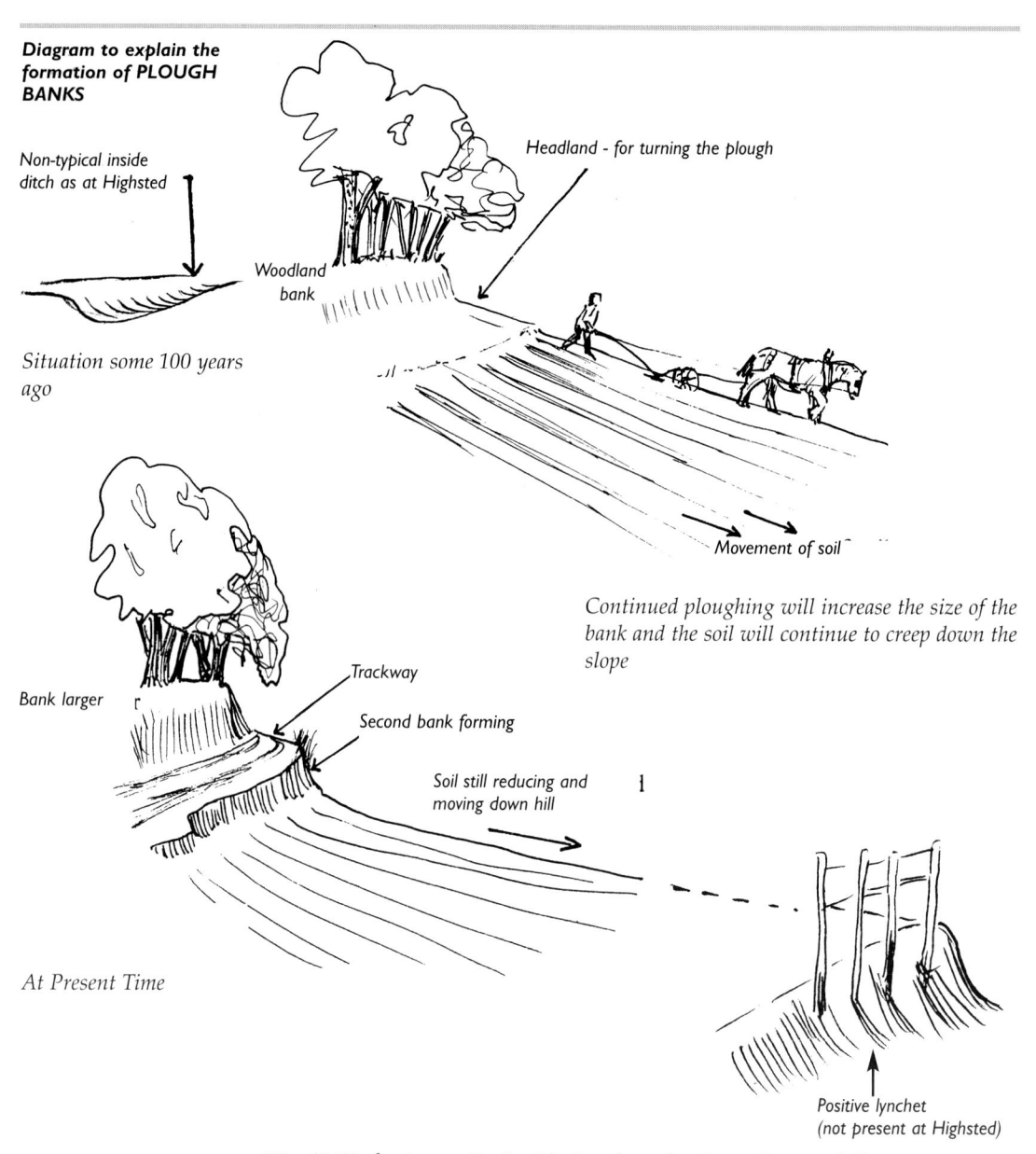

Wood? He had not. So I added rather slowly and regretfully "A great pity, because you would have found a hollow way and bank as large as the one you have just shown."

BUT if the situation had occured as in the illustration and a negative lynchet (as it is called) had been formed by the plough (= the woodland bank) *then* there should be a positive lynchet (banking up of the plough soil) at the foot of the field, *and* in the Highsted field *that has not happened!* Also the inside ditch is not typical. So all in all the archaeologist should have looked more closely and certainly walked the whole site.

The 'Plough Banks' theory could have been a genuine mistake, but another archaeologist told a friend of mine that they had *"dug all the sites of interest in the Sittingbourne area"*. Implying that there could be nothing on Highsted Farm!

The barrage of comments continued and the 'putting off' messages seemed firm, clear, and rather upsetting. I was told I should *"Follow professional advice and leave Highsted alone"*. I was so non-plussed by that one, I wrote back and asked which 'professionals', for the Directors of Canterbury and Thanet Archaeological Trusts had always been encouraging and had never said that.

Yet another comment coming from the same person as the previous one was :-

"Ancient sites are best left alone!" But as he was obviously unaware of these sites it struck me as a very head-in-the-sand attitude! Did he imply they should be left to the plough to destroy? What the eye does not see the heart does not grieve over! Still another, who walked the site with me, tried to put me off, everything I showed him he had some other explanation for! I could see that his arguments were *possible* but there were far too many clues pointing to the presence of a major site rather than an absence. For instance, we had found quite a few geode stones which are spherical flints ideal for use as missiles, sling shots! He insisted they were 'natural' and therefore could be disregarded.

Granted they *are* natural and often have a quartz formation inside them ....but Iron Age people *did* collect them and I knew some had been listed as being found in the 1955 grave sites. Much later when we had found a total of over a hundred, I wrote a message on one of them and sent it to him! Meeting him last year I finally knew he had forgiven my cryptic sense of humour, and bygones are bygones!

(If you look in *"Iron Age Britain"* English Heritage book by B. Cunliffe, p.92. there is a picture of sling shots being used).

A bone was found on the northern edge of the bank. It appeared to be very old as it was crumbling. Soon after it was found I showed it to Dr. Birch who had worked on the original bone finds of 1955. He said it resembled the condition they were in and it *could* be human but he was doubtful.

"Oh, its not necessarily old and not human, a sheep or pig," someone tried to brush me off with. I remained quiet, thinking to myself, my mammalian Zoology is a little rusty but that's a heck of a tall sheep! I thought some more .....if he says it is not old ....and Dr. Birch said it *could* be human ......I had better send it to the Coroner!

So it went to the Gillingham Coroner (Medway Towns) via Sittingbourne Police Station. Back it came with a kindly note from the Coroner:-

"Not Human. But very old, back into antiquity!"

My vet finally solved the problem, it is the cannon bone of a horse, some 15 hands high.

So is it the missing horse found Circa 1920 when they were hand digging at the start of Quarry II? It would make sense that someone re-buried it in what was then the edge of Highsted Wood.

If you look carefully the dents on either side are where the missing splint bones are found. Splint bones are the remnants of the horses other toes ...it only walks on one toe, not two, like a sheep.

In 1986 I had taken some of my finds into a museum, and the curator was at

Left: Cannon bone of a horse @ 15 hands high found on the edge of the north bank.

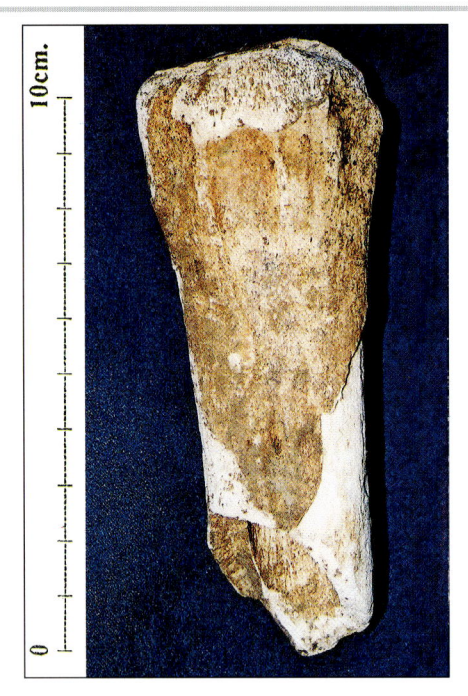

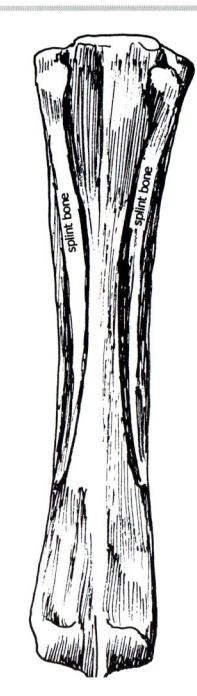

Right: Diagram of a complete cannon bone.

first very interested. Then when I said the northern end of the site had a *square* banking system he said very hastily *"Well then it cannot be Celtic, they are never square!"*

I repeated this comment to Clare Curran in 1996 and she said exactly the same as I had thought ....sometimes they are square if they are of religious significance.

The large chunk of Iron Slag I had shown to this same Museum Curator .....and he made no comment! Yet I knew iron slag was reasonably uncommon in that part of Kent. (See page 23) As we were coming out or the museum my elder daughter, who was then 15, said *"Mum, that was a complete waste of time, he was just not interested!"*

One comment that is a typical *"wool-over-the-eyes"* saying that tends to discourage people from looking for more evidence of sites, is the one that dismisses pottery sherds as having *"fallen -off-the-back-of-a-dung-cart!"*

The reasoning behind this theory is that broken pots were ignominiously thrown on the dung heap in the farmyard and then when the manure was spread on the fields they became scattered. Yet this ignores the fact that to get numerous broken sherds in one field location there must have been an equivalent farm-yard very near by to supply the dung + sherds! It may work as a theory for the odd sherd but not when one has a great *selection* of sherds of different ages in one location (as in the 'ditch' context of Highsted Farm). It also has less validity than the supposition that sites are indeed very frequent in rural Kent (Caesar tells us there were houses *"everywhere"*) and the problem is that ancient houses and everything else has become churned up in the top soil. If one finds sherds of different ages and with little abrasion (cleanly broken edges with no wear) as with some of the Highsted sherds, *then* one is closer to assuming there is a site that *has not been ploughed* to any extent and evidence of the houses will hopefully be there.

The most hurtful comment of all and one I find harder to laugh at, was one from someone who I thought was a friend :-

"You amateurs breeze in thinking your sites are important!"

It really took me aback, for everything flashed through my mind. Did he mean some other amateurs as well who had found some very interesting items on other sites we had been to see together? I thought he was being very unfair! Besides, the comment is statistically invalid! For there are so many sites 'missing' or 'mislaid' in the area of Kent I have been looking at that to fit the estimated statistic for the rest of southern England of "one site for every quarter mile", if an 'amateur' returns finds/evidence then the site is quite likely to be important!

I have had so much encouragement and help from very enthusiastic archaeologists since then ...hence this book! Even the four page criticism of an article and how "amateurishly" I had written it and made the drawings .....from someone who has now passed on ..... I ignore (he must just have been in a bad mood or so I have been told!)

(To improve your drawing techniques see "Drawing Archaeological Finds" by N. Griffiths, A. Jenner & C. Wilson)

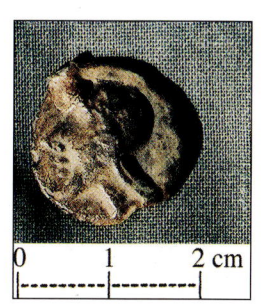

How I draw or paint items or write .....is now my own style. I only hope you enjoy reading this book and find it interesting, for that is what it is written for! Hopefully I have not made *too* many mistakes and some people will be encouraged to do their own archaeological projects.

Fortunately, balancing all the negativeness I have encountered in Kent is a very *positive* attitude towards amateur archaeologists, particularly in Sussex. The Sussex Archaeology Society organises an archaeological forum to which representatives of all groups, amateur and professional, can attend to discuss recent findings and projects in the County. The 'amateur' Hastings Area Archaeology Group is very active and I have been a member for some twenty years. (See Chapter 15). The East Sussex County Archaeologist has organised and taken part in a very successful and on going dig at Glossam's Place in Beckley Wood for the past three years (1999-2001). It is proving to be a very interesting medieval moated site with an underlying Romano-British iron works.

The efforts of HAARG diggers were also rewarded this last year in a successful dig in a Hastings backyard with an amazing haul of finds. (Again see chapter 15.)

Archaeology should be of interest to farmers, dowsers, biologists, physicists, ley hunters et al with everyone contributing thoughts, information, and expertise to solve certain enigmas and problems. Archaeology by its very nature is a study and domain of all.

No more scoffing and off-putting please, from anyone ....archaeology should be fun!

And there is so much still to find, record and add to our knowledge, particularly in Kent!

As if to confirm this last line, whilst I was completing this chapter a superb Iron Age coin was turned up near Lenham by a metal detector surveying our new Community Centre site. One would assume that there was little archaeology there at all when none at all showed in the sub soil sampling last October (and I watched every trench very carefully) but at some time approximately 2000 years ago a Celt, presumably of the Catuvellauni tribe who minted it, dropped this coin, a potin of Thurrock type.

Highsted banks at the north-west corner, looking south.

It is notoriously difficult to show a banking system clearly on photographs. Contours seem to flatten out. The above panorama is the double-banked square ended enclosure viewed from the north west in 1992, the white house just visible under the branches of the left hand cherry tree is where this second much older photograph (circa 1935) was taken from. The parch marks of the outer valleculae are behind the photographer and were only noticed towards the end of the dig.

In 1996 we had to decide where to dig and it seemed sensible to drop a long narrow trench across the banks just to the left of the central cherry tree. (Its die-back is just starting, by 1998 it had died completely and by then the newly planted cordon apple trees were well established).

By 1992 the ditch running along the inside of the main bank was no longer visible.

View at Highsted, looking north west from Stockers Hill.

In the left hand upper field two slightly darker bands seem to indicate that the banks were once present on the southern side. In 1935 the main enclosure was still under woodland (as can be seen, top right) the cherry orchard just above the farm cottages is where the roman tile and sherds have been retrieved. The young orchard in the left distance is where many pieces of iron slag and worked flints have been found.

Permission for the dig was kindly given by Garth Doubleday and Edmund Doubleday, the owners of Highsted Farm.

Chapter 6
The First Dig, 1996

We did not seem to be getting many definitive answers as to the exact nature of the banks and 'settlement' area. In 1994, members of Maidstone Area Archaeology Group (M.A.A.G.) did some auger hole investigations that suggested that the main bank was clay. The inside ditch by then had already been disrupted and there seemed to be little evidence in the soil samples that it had even been there! It seemed that to find out more we would have to do a dig!

After my daughter, Beena, graduated from Exeter University with a degree in Archaeology she and another Exeter graduate, Clare Curran, helped conduct an excavation in the summer of 1996.

To help us to see the best places to start we had a geophysical survey done by a firm from Oxford, Bartlett-Clark Consultancy. (See the print out p.51).

The area of the ditch seemed to be well and truly disrupted by the changes made to the orchard and as there were young trees already planted we had agreed with Garth Doubleday to restrict our excavation to areas west of the fence line. Even so, by our calculations and viewing the 1985 photograph, trench II should have been through this important 'ditch' area. As the mechanical digger took off the turf for us a piece of Beaker pottery was found. In fact it might have been better that we had not used a digger at all, because we found that archaelogical prehistoric evidence and pottery was present just under the surface. (As I explained in Chapter 3 this seems to be common in rural areas). Trench II showed no evidence of soil colour change that would indicate the ditch was present (i.e. darker soil in the fill). But I will add here that despite failure to find the ditch either by excavation or in the geophysical survey it did show with dowsing!

Or rather an indication of water showed with dowsing. Even just ten years ago I would have been castigated for even mentioning the possibilities of dowsing! (Read my scientific explanation in Chapter 10). In this case it was very genuine. A young 11 year old girl on site, daughter of a Head Master, (who used to live in Highsted Cottages in 1955) was given a freshly cut hazel twig by her father and shown how to hold it. I watched slightly bemused because she was so sceptical and determined that she was not going to be 'fooled' by anything. As she walked slowly across the the ditch area of Trench II, the twig twisted out of her grip so violently that she yelled as it stung her hand.

Perhaps we had not dug deeply enough and the hard packed clay we had come to was not the bottom 'natural' subsoil. As this was late on in the dig and we had started to backfill ...it would be advisable on another occasion (if that is possible) to try again!

Even so this particular trench yielded five pieces of Belgic grog ware, one piece of Beaker (extremely rare), a piece of Bronze Age pottery, two pieces of sandy Roman ware, two rim pieces of shell tempered Roman, grey smooth rim of Upchurch ware (Roman) and a piece of base of mock Samian, (Roman).

So it had an amazing spread of ages (3000 years) in a fairly small area.

Trench I was more successful. It was decided to cut it down over the banking system near the N.W. corner of the site. This area showed on Alister Bartlett's geophys as having an area of magnetic disturbance. It appears from our excavation that that area is a layer of chalk. Two shallow post holes showed in this surface and a piece of Neolithic pottery and two worked flints were found

Two worked flints found in a post hole in Trench I

in one. Another piece of Neolithic pottery was found in the chalk context. There were two cart ruts crossing this chalk surface ....that <u>might</u> suggest it was a trackway at some time (more investigation is needed!)

The main bank above this chalk area consisted of clay (as also found by the auger holes in 1994). But a line of very large flint nodules was discovered running parallel to the bank and helping to structure it. Careful examination determined that these flints continued for some way along the bank for they broke through the grass in many places.

This use of flint nodules in the banks is common in this area of Kent. There are similar ones on Oak Tree Farm across the Highsted Valley and large flints also border many fields and orchards and the fact they run in a NE → SW direction may be further residual proof of a reave system. (See page 36)

Whether the chalk layer extends as a rectangle, (as vaguely suggested by the geophysical survey). is unclear (again more excavation would be needed to confirm this possiblity). But it is unlikely that the layer is 'natural' it is way above the level of the chalk in the quarry and we did not encounter it in the 1998 excavation further down the slope in a trench cut in the same directional line.

Neolithic sherds. 1&2 from Trench I post holes. Depth of context was only 25cm below the surface! 3rd from Trench III

Photographs of Woodstock Sherds found in 1996

A = 'Belgic' grog ware
B = Beaker sherd
C = Late Bronze Age
D = Roman, mock Samian base

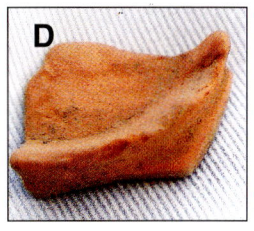

A third trench was cut across another small square bank ...but little showed except that the bank was of fine clay: although one further piece of Neolithic pottery was retrieved .

The shallowness of the contexts is a very important find in itself. So many archaeologists seem to think old contexts (such as this apparent Neolithic surface) should be under feet of soil! I explained the reason why that is often not so in Chapter. 3, page 22.

Three sherds from the "lost Ditch" area of Highsted and their possible pot forms. These sherds demonstrate the huge time spread of this area of the site from Bronze Age to Roman.

A = Early Beaker
B = 'Belgic' grog ware
C = Grey Upchurch ware, Roman

1996 Excavation:- Trench 1

Width = 1m.

When we looked in the woodland area it was clear that the ancient wood had very little depth of soil either and that had never been ploughed! The woodland had about 5cm. of leaf litter overlaying just 15 cm. of top soil.

So ancient sites are very fragile indeed, especially when on hills or slopes. Even to say that they are "safe" under orchard or woodland is not true. In modern coppicing the ruts from large wheeled tractors often churn up the surface no end.

Towards the end of the two week dig everyone was getting a little despondent that no real definitive items had appeared (bar the sherds) and that we had failed to find the top ditch. Then as we were sitting by the camp fire having tea I suddenly noticed the vegetation. *"There is a ditch over there!"* I said, *"Look at the lush growth of the grass!"*

On closer examination we all thought there could be two ditches and two banks, possibly three! The explanation of the parch marks (caused by poor soil and dry conditions for the grass roots) is shown in this diagram :-

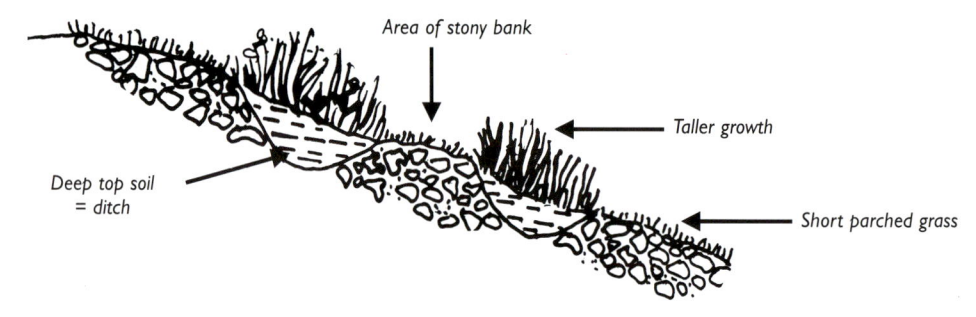

The actual photograph of the parch mark taken the next day.

After noticing these parch marks we did some auger holes in the 'ditch' areas and the soil was at least 1m. in depth (screw was not long enough to get to the bottom!)

So to make sure we called Alister Bartlett back to do an additional survey of this area.

When David Perkins, the Director of Thanet Archaeological Trust saw our sherds from the dig and saw this photograph, he said very slowly and deliberately **"You must section those banks and ditches!"** It was then that I took a course at Sussex University on Practical Archaeology .... but it was not till 1996 that an opportunity arose for the second dig.

Highsted, Kent; Geophysical Survey 1996
Plan 2: Resistivity Survey (Positive anomolies shaded, 'ditch' marked with green lines)
Surveyed by:
Bartlett-Clark Consultancy
Specialists in Archaeogeophysics
This is the area that needed sectioning!

The main "team" in 1996, Beena Patel, Clare Curran and Alastair Hawkins.

51

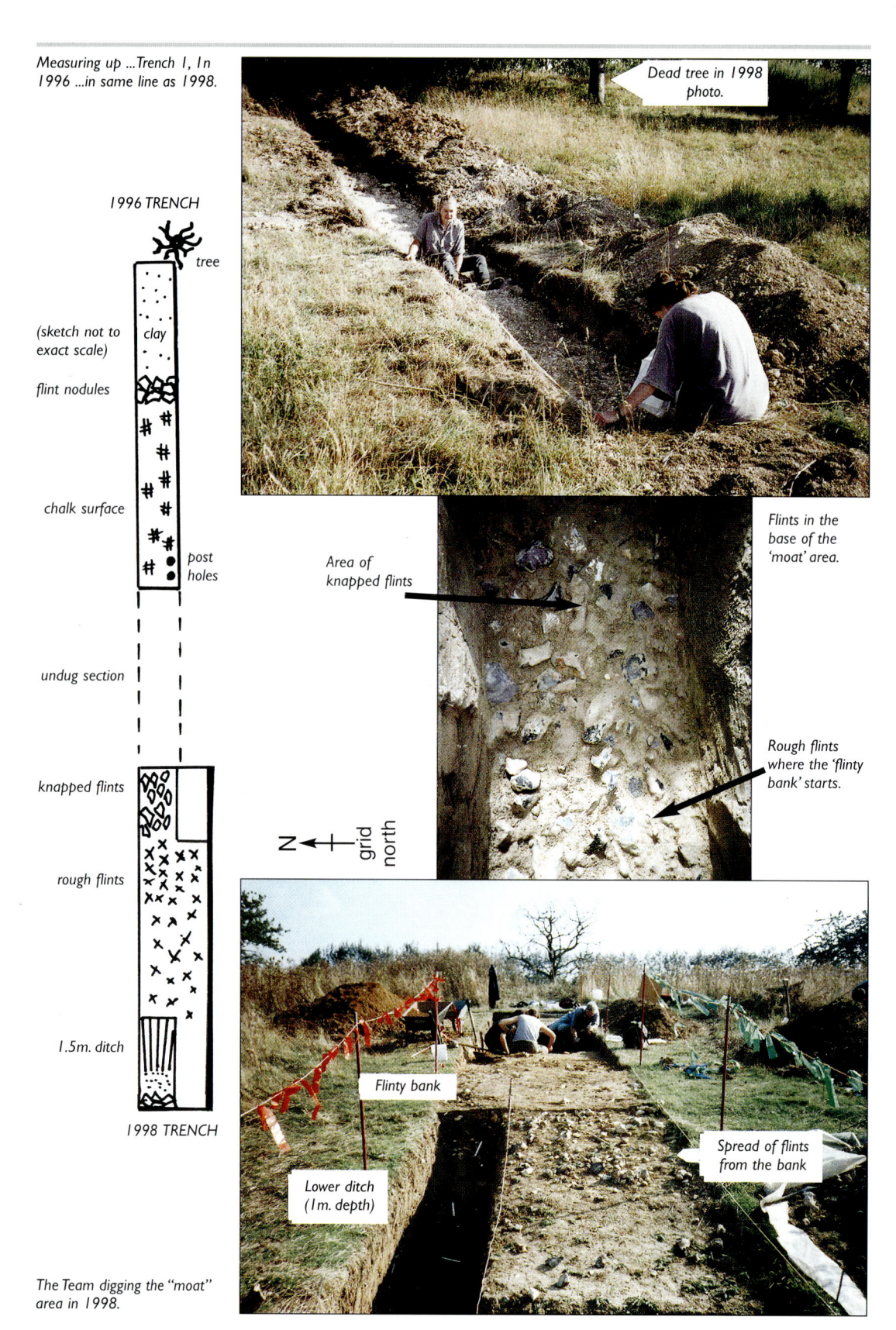

Measuring up ...Trench 1, In 1996 ...in same line as 1998.

Dead tree in 1998 photo.

1996 TRENCH

tree

(sketch not to exact scale)

clay

flint nodules

chalk surface

post holes

undug section

knapped flints

rough flints

1.5m. ditch

1998 TRENCH

Flints in the base of the 'moat' area.

Area of knapped flints

Rough flints where the 'flinty bank' starts.

N ← grid north

Flinty bank

Spread of flints from the bank

Lower ditch (1m. depth)

The Team digging the "moat" area in 1998.

52

Chapter 7

The Second Dig, 1998

In 1997 I had obtained a Certificate in Practical Archaeology from the University of Sussex in a series of evening and week-end courses, this helped me to be more confident to help conduct a dig to section the possible banks and ditches on the site. The opportunity to do this arose in 1998 when Lower Medway Archaeological Research Group (L.M.A.R.G.) needed a site for a proposed training dig.

"Earth feet, loam feet lifted in country mirth
Mirth of those long since under the earth"

A professional archaeologist who was quite encouraging, looked at my notes, and said we did indeed have an Iron Age settlement site. He suggested we sectioned using a mechanical excavator as there was a lot of soil to shift! On hindsight this would have been the most successful way, but as we wanted to use the excavation to show younger members how it should be done in the more 'classic' way using manual digging we opted for the slower approach!

We opened a 2 metre wide, 15 metre long trench down across the parch marks (still visible as differences in growth). Care was taken to align it with the Trench I cut in 1996. Conveniently we could find the same cherry tree! We also consulted the geophysical printout to make sure we sliced through the area of the possible ditch.

Even when just the turf had been removed, the stony area of the middle bank was obvious. Stones from this bank area had tumbled down across what should have been the ditch. A metre wide section was dug on the northern edge of the main trench and the in-fill of the ditch carefully removed. This ditch was 1m.deep and the fill was a mixture of top-soil and layers of clay, with a few flints but not many .The base seemed to be flint and gravel. Few finds appeared in this 'fill' at all, but there were three pieces of ancient pot (Bronze Age and Iron Age) and three pieces of very thin bubbled filled glass that indicated they were a very old form, possibly Roman.

David Cox, one of the Lower Medway Group members thought at first that the glass claw was part of a Saxon glass vessel, but this earlier Roman find just 2

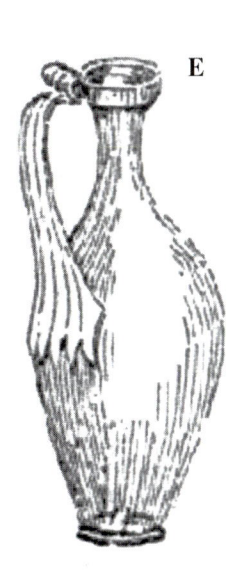

A=glass 'claw' that is similar to claws on E.
B&C = very thin pieces of aqua glass.
D&E =blue glass phials found in a Roman lead coffin in Milton, near Sittingbourne in 1868, see 'Collectanea Antiqua' Vol.6.

53

Sectional plan of Highsted Banking System

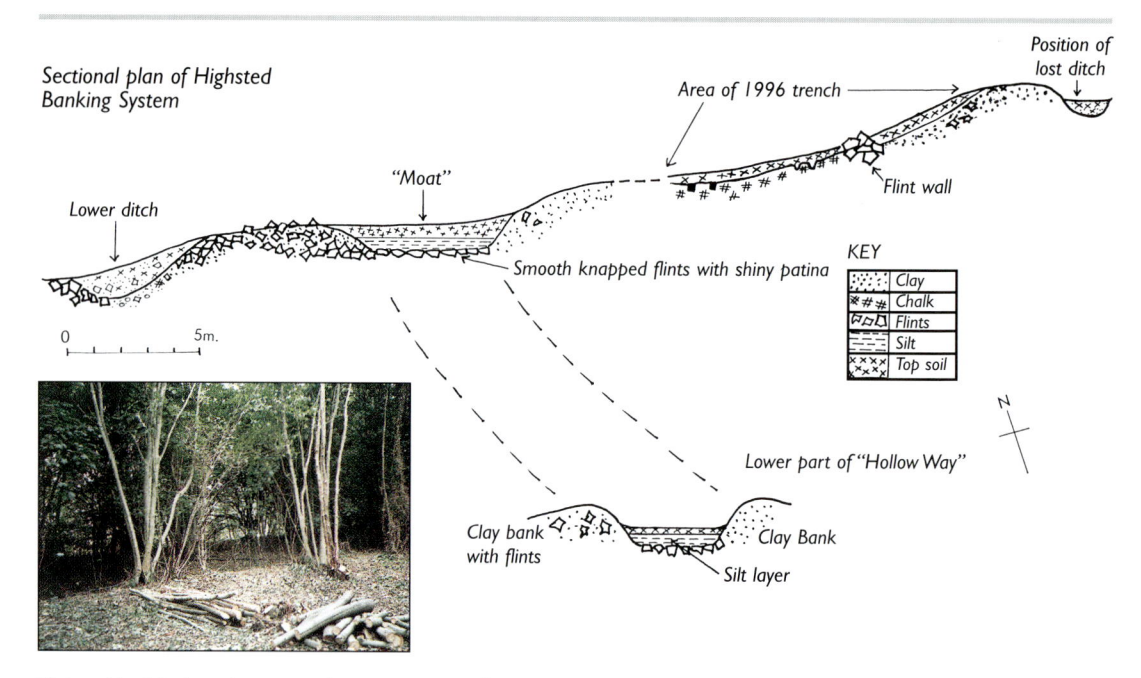

Photograph of the lower part of the "Hollow Way" in the wood.

miles distant might confirm it is indeed Roman. Our glass finds also back up earlier reports we had from local people that *'Roman blue glass'* was found when the woodland was 'stumped' in the late 1930's to make the orchard; and reports of similar glassware when Cromer's Road was cut in the late 1920's.

The area above the stony bank (where the parch mark indicated another ditch) was at first thought to be 'just clay' but persistence in digging through this layer indicated that it was silt, either washed down from the higher bank above, or could it be alluvial fill? The latter suggestion seemed a possibility, as there were 'eddies' of fine grit and rolled chalk granules just as one might find at the bottom of a stream. Finally it was discovered the silt was lying above a flat layer of flints. These flints extended towards and formed part of the 'stony bank' but they were different in the two regions. Under the silt they were knapped off and smooth and shiny. The shiny patina was consistent with the orange/green/or blue patina found on flints that had been long in contact with water. In the area where logically there should have been a retaining coffer bank, the flints were rough, pointed and with their external cortex still intact. (i.e. they had not been knapped)

But in the area of the sheared off or knapped flints, wedged between these, were a few flints that could possibly be worked flint flakes but their edges had been rolled and damaged (by tumbling around in a stream?).

The layer of silt appeared to be on the same level as the hollow way as it curved out of the wood towards the orchard. Consequently, it was necessary to investigate the hollow way a little more to establish if there was a relationship. Trial holes were dug, one in each of the banks and one in the centre of the Hollow way. The hollow central area was filled with 30cm. of fine silt over-lying a layer of flints ....that were similar to those found in the upper ditch area, for they appeared to be knapped off in the same 'cobble' fashion. (See the drawings) The outermost bank was clay with considerable numbers of flints reinforcing it (equivalent to the bank between the two ditch areas of our main trench?) The innermost bank was clay with very few flints (again matching the innermost bank of the main trench.)

If this was a flint track-way then it is likely that the knapping could have occurred from horses' hooves, but what of the layer of silt? Could it possibly have been a moat? I phoned up one of my tutors in Sussex, *"Have any moats older than medieval ever been found?"* I asked. *"No"* he replied firmly but then he added *"But that does not mean to say that there weren't any. Make sure that you try and find evidence at the bottom of both the ditches and the banks that might establish the age."*

That has been the elusive proof! Samples of soil were taken from the bottom of both ditches and the hollow way but little organic matter had survived the clay's acidity, and no definitive items were found! Much more excavation is needed!

Strangely, very few sherds were found and those that appeared other than the ancient ones were 19th-20th century. Were the ditches filled in those centuries? Areas cut out from the main bank further along in the cherry orchard, might suggest that soil was taken for that purpose.

Evidence of the retaining bank for the 'moat' in the section we were digging was not strong. It appeared that the clay with flint retaining bank (as in the outer one of the hollow way) had been removed when the ditches were filled. Look at the sectional drawing to see the possible structure and a quick sketch to explain what likely happened is drawn here:-

It was disappointing that we did not find more items to confirm that the ditch and bank system was indeed ancient but the few scraps of pottery and ancient glass tend to suggest that it was. Hopefully, a group of local keen archaeologists can be inspired to have another organised dig to find out?

Did the eminent and very active archaeologist George Payne, F.S.A., excavate and fill these ditches circa 1890? He was asked to remove the tumulus at Woodstock house by the owner, Mr. Twopenny, and it is quite possible he was also asked to flatten these vallecullae. (As banks and ditches are sometimes termed.)

I have researched George Payne's notes in the Guildhall Museum in Rochester but he does not mention these banks at Highsted/Woodstock at all. But that does not necessarily mean he was unaware of them or that they were not there even then – he might have found so little evidence *"just a few pieces of rude pottery"* was one of his favourite descriptions. If more extensive notes of his ever emerge, perhaps the puzzle about the Woodstock banks might be solved. Here is George Payne's description of the tumulus from his book *"Collectanea Cantiana"* 1893:-

"It was anticipated that Woodstock would have furnished some clue to its early history, when a large 'tumulus' was opened in Cromer's Wood on 29th July1881, by order of the owner of the estate, the late Edward Twopenny, Esq., who invited the writer to conduct the excavations. The mound was circular in form and surrounded by a well-defined fosse seventy-one paces round, it measured nineteen paces over the apex from one ditch to the other, and occupied a prominent position to the south-east of Woodstock House, and not far in the wood which slopes down to the Sittingbourne and Wormshill or Frinsted road. The digging proceeded slowly, as the 'tumulus' was composed almost wholly of flint stones gathered from the hill-side; trenches were cut completely through to the base from the east to the west and north to south. Finding nothing but a few pieces of pottery of uncertain date and a flint chipped into the shape of a ball, we trenched the four quarters left, and finally cleared away the mound entirely; after which we dug out the base to a depth of two feet to make sure of leaving nothing behind. The work of destruction took nearly a fortnight to accomplish, with unfortunately a negative result, at which I was greatly disappointed as Mr.Twopenny and the members of his family had evinced such keen interest in the work."

Similar hammer stone from below Rumstead near Stockbury.

He goes on to say *"The flint ball found in the mound is exactly similar to one discovered at Grovehurst. These balls appear to have derived their spherical form from being used as hammer stones, they are evenly chipped all over their surfaces, the angles having been worn off by continual use."….."It is probable that the Woodstock tumulus had at some time been rifled of its contents, as there was a very noticeable depression on its summit, and curiously enough, below this, we found the fragments of pottery of doubtful age."*

So the likelihood that George Payne (or someone else) was asked to flatten the banks around Woodstock remains. Certainly our few ancient samples of pottery and glass and the few pieces of modern crockery in the ditch fill suggests that that is the case.

Our excavation of Woodstock has come to a standstill, unless someone else can be inspired to take up the trowel and discover more?

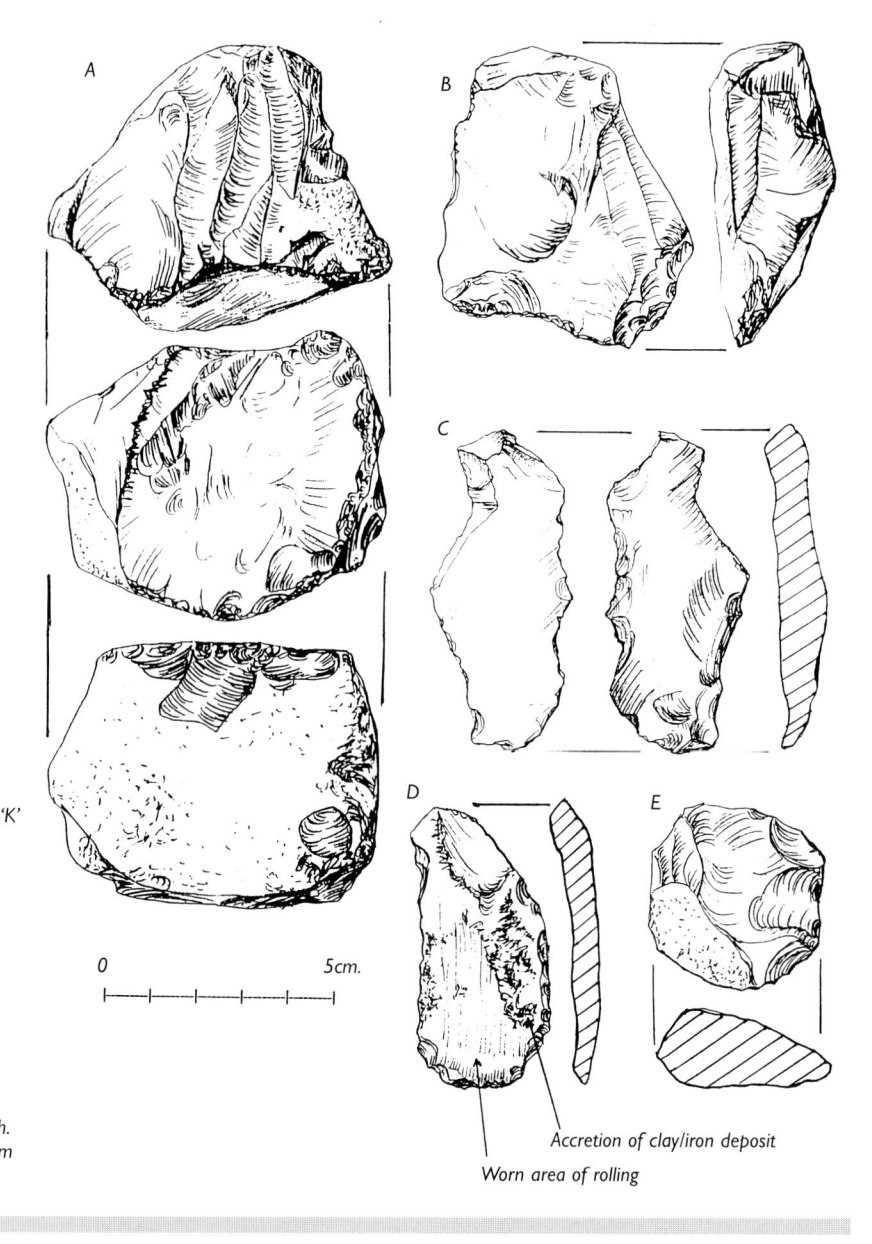

A = Cobbled flint from area 'K' in the wood at a depth of 30cm, under raw sienna coloured silt.
B = highly polished surface with a bright burnt-sienna patina. Typical of many carpetting the area at 'J'. All were with shiny side uppermost.
C & D = blade flakes with limited secondary working. Found wedged between the "cobbles" of the 1998 trench.
E = another worked flint from 'J'. (see plan on page 12)

Accretion of clay/iron deposit

Worn area of rolling

Chapter 8

Assessment, Mystery Solved?

Personally I think it is pretty obvious that there is an ancient site extending from the parch mark banks and ditches near the edge of the Highsted quarry across to the woodland bank still visible in part at Woodstock on the Broad Oak road.*

The evidence can now be listed as :-

1. The proximity of the 26 graves found in 1955, (mostly aligned so that the occupants were facing their home).

2. The Bronze Age axe found in 1927, 200metres distant on Ruins Barn road.

3. The pottery sherds of so many different eras found in the ditch area:- Bronze Age, Beaker, 'Belgic'grog ware, Roman Upchurch ware, Roman sandy ware, Roman mock Samian .

4. Selection of worked flints:- Mesolithic, Neolithic and possibly Bronze Age.

5. Three sherds of Neolithic pottery (2 found in context of a post hole). This may not sound many but Neolithic pottery is an extremely rare find …as is Beaker.

6. Chalk surface that appears to be Neolithic (more excavation needed!)

7. Around 100 sling shots (natural geode stones amassed as ammunition.)

8. Presence of Romano-British iron slag.

9. Three scraps of thin, aqua, bubbled filled glass, one in particular matching finds of Roman glass at nearby Milton .

10. Last, and not least the banking system itself and particularly the inside ditch as featured in the 1985 photograph.

> "Under the days declining beam and call
> Images and memories from ruin or from ancient trees
> For I would ask a question of them all" W.B.Yeats

* My next door neighbour has just told me he used to work at Woodstock Research Centre and he had noticed banks and ditches showing across there also! Now I have provided him with an explanaion of what he had observed.

In November 2000 we have been reminded in Great Britain of how wet our climate can be. It is thought that in the Bronze Age and Iron Ages it was quite wet and in Roman times certainly even warmer than now, when grapes were grown in the Doddington Valley, approximately where a new vineyard has just been planted. So 'global warming' is not new! It is thought that the sea levels in Roman times were *higher* than now, certainly on the south coast. (Although the land level has risen in Scotland since then and gives the impression the sea has *lowered* there.)

Sea levels and water tables are a complicated issue that I do not wish to debate here in detail, BUT the wetter climate is important when one considers banks and ditches on a clay subsoil. It is quite obvious to me that they would fill with water and with just a little care with pugging, they could be made to be a permanent feature.

Why it is rarely suggested that Iron Age sites had water filled ditches I can never understand. I even have my doubts that all the moated sites were

Typical Irish crannog

HIGHSTED

Possible scenario circa B.C.50
Was it the settlement that gave Woodstock its name?
Did the ditches on clay subsoil, hold water?
Totems = artistic licence! (Post holes not)

Quercus petraea = Swamp oak/sessile oak
Likes water, grows far larger than **Q. robur**.
Could it have been grown on sacred sites for use in boat building?
It still grows on Highsted.

Chalk surface

Rodmersham

Golden Wood

Constitution Hill
N.A. Axe

Tonge Castle
(originally N.A.)

Highsted R.

Burial ground

Woodland is still very damp.
Juncus effusus - soft rush
Juncus Bufonious - toad rush are still very prolific

Woodstock Stream
(tributary of Highsted R.)

View looking NE

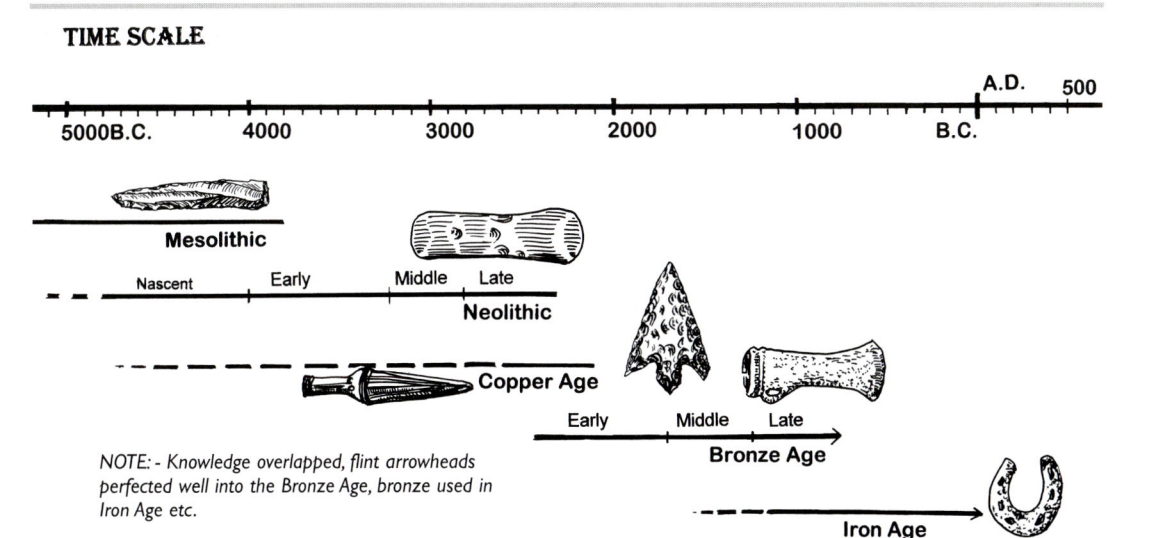

TIME SCALE

For those not familiar with the time scale of the various Ages here is a simple table:-

originally 'Medieval' and the thought has often occurred to me that they were built on existing far older sites!

If Bronze Age people favoured lake villages ….is it not logical that they surrounded themselves with water wherever possible?

And following on from there, Iron Age people could have done the same, but possibly, more from a defensive point of view. Medieval moated sites may just have been a rehash of a well-known, ancient, traditional method of settlement, particularly in the wet areas of the Weald of Kent. Cranogs, in Ireland are a similar parallel and some show habitation from Neolithic through to Medieval.

Last century (it sounds strange to use that term for the 1960's) P. J. Tester excavated a Roman Villa in Cobham Park. He went on to cut an exploratory trench through the adjacent earthwork. He never got to the bottom of the ditch because his trench filled up with water! In the 1960's we also had some rather wet weather …and what was I saying about ditches on clay? But the pity is he then categorically said the site was <u>definitely</u> not ancient ….I just think that site should be looked at again because clay creeps so much and finding some medieval tile does not necessarily rule out there was a more ancient site there in the first place! (see *Archaeologia Cantiana* vol. 76. 1961 and map p.114)

I am not claiming I am categorically right on the 'water filled' ditch theory at Woodstock, but am putting it forward as a logical argument. Hence my reconstruction drawing featured in this chapter and on the cover.

To work out exactly what Highsted/Woodstock was like in each millennium is a daunting task. It needs a lot more investigation and excavation.

Surveying on Highsted farm In 1998.

Terry Heaslip (MAAG)
Matthew Heaslip (MAAG)
Dana Adler (Chair of LMARG)
Roger Wallbridge (MAAG)
David Carder (MAAG & LMARG)

We just scratched at the surface ….but it would have been nice if we had had more backing and support from various groups. For instance, we needed to borrow a dumpy level to survey the site. I eventually borrowed one from the Hastings group (not even our County). I had requested borrowing one from Kent Archaeological Society and was told that they used to lend them out but as one came back damaged they retracted the service! I wondered, casually, whether insurance was ever a consideration?

Looking at the evidence we had found:- it certainly did appear that the silt layer of the upper ditch was caused by water, either standing or slowly moving (evidenced by the eddies of particles) the retaining bank was largely missing, but it is present in the hollow way in the wood.

So mysteries remain!

Have we found evidence of an ancient moated site, originally Neolithic then superimposed with Bronze Age/Beaker/Iron Age and Romano-British?

Was the Neolithic originally a causewayed enclosure?

Are the hollows in the woodland area hut dwellings?

Is the rectangular area of magnetic disturbance (showing on the geophysical survey) and apparently corresponding with the chalk area …a Neolithic Longhouse? Or just a natural area of chalk? Or is it something else?

Was the square banked area with the inside ditch, once a sanctuary? That is a more difficult query to solve as there has now been so much disruption in that area. But it may have been an area of industry, the iron slag, possible iron ingot and even the presence of glass may indicate that these were made there.

The overall assessment from the evidence gathered is that Woodstock represents a very ancient site with possible continuous use from Mesolithic through to Romano-British. The banking system seems to include a water filled ditch that encircled the north-western side of the site. The 'hollow way' appears to be one of the ditches between the banks as they curve around to a possible western gateway. The main causeway approach seems to have been lost in farming the arable field to the south of the site. The beautiful woodland 'dell', present as a feature till the 1960's, seems to have been filled in with rubbish by Shell Research.

2001 View of Woodstock banking system looking South to where the Dell (West Gate?) used to be.

Line drawing to help with interpretation

It seems strange that it was allowed as a land fill site and one wonders (hopes!) that no waste from the Research Centre was buried there! Would the hollows either side of Maidencastle gateway ever be allowed as 'land fill'? I think not, so how was this allowed without a thorough archaeological survey ……...?

There are possibly, many more sites in the Sittingbourne to Lenham areas and I find it a great mystery that more people have not looked!

In the "settlement dynamics" (see page 116) there seem to be great comparisons to be made between three sites Woodstock, White Horse (Blue Bell Hill) and Snarkhurst (Hollingbourne):-

1. They are all on low ridges/hills that are not the highest point of the Downs. (Defensive hill-forts may have overlooked them all.)
2. All have associated barrow/sacred sites.
3. All had iron workings.
4. All show continuous habitation from Neolithic Romano-British.
5. All had adjacent 'sacred' springs or streams.
6. Did they all have bronze workings? White Horse certainly did. Was this a 'sacred' task also?
7. All three need a lot more investigation!

Chapter 9

The Chalk Pit Eden, and other Wildlife

This chapter is not meant to be a complete survey of all the wildlife of the area but a brief description of the most prominent and of specific interest.

The most dominant ecological feature that hits one when visiting the site are the chalk quarries. The largest, Chalk Pit II, ran out of space in the mid 1950's. The Cement Company then tunnelled under Cromer's road and made Chalk Pit III. That ceased production in 1962.

From its southern end (the newest) to the tunnel there is a gradation of re-colonisation.

> *" How pleasant thy banks and green valley below, Where wild in the woodlands the primroses blow."*
> *"Sweet Afton" by R. Burns*

Walnut Tree :-

One can speculate how some species manage to grow in such unlikely situations but one of the oldest trees in the new habitat of the abandoned Chalk Pit III is a walnut tree growing near the Cromer's Road face. Did someone lob a nut over from the roadway or did someone have a picnic and throw away a nut they could not crack?

Or did a long abandoned and buried nut finally germinate from disturbed top soil?

Whatever the origin it is now a flourishing tree. Its growth cannot be older than 46 years ....when the quarry was first started.

The southern end of the quarry is still relatively barren with very few species gaining a hold. Birch trees are the commonest, as one can see in the photograph. Where there was a shute of top soil down the cliff face, there are far more trees and variety of plants growing. One such shute can be seen across Chalk Pit II in the newspaper pictures of Chapter 2 and is invaluable to exactly pinpoint where the graves were located.

View of Chalk Pit III from its S.W. corner. Note the present water-table ponds in the bottom of the quarry.

Bee Orchid - Ophrys apifera & Twayblade - Listeria ovata.

Orchids

One of the most stunning aspects of Chalk Pit III is the speed of recolonisation and the presence in early summer of so many orchids. Their minute seeds, as fine as fungus spores germinate amongst the crushed chalk and flinty gravel. The high calcium levels favour their growth. In 1996 there was a host of bee orchids, the next year apparently few at all ....but that is typical and they seem to have years of profusion then few the next.

The tunnel through to Quarry II from Quarry III. There was a rail track through here.

The common twayblade is certainly common there and its aptly named leaf in two neat sections are noticeable even before the greenish yellow flower spike emerges from between them in mid June.

The common spotted orchid seems to be a universal inhabitant and is common in Chalk Pit II as well. The southern marsh orchid apparently grows in Chalk Pit 1. *(Daetylorchis praetermissa).*

I have not explored all the vast terrain of Chalk Pit II but it presents a unique quiet, peaceful area, a kind of 'lost world'. It is a strange sensation to stand on its neatly grazed glades and look up at the chalk face towering above and speculate that one is standing **below** the position of those long lost barrows.

Rabbits :-

The tightly grazed grass is the result of a vast colony of rabbits, their evidence made plain by the frequent piles of dung pellets on their favourite knolls and vantage points. They act as efficient lawn mowers and unfortunately have a taste for a great variety of plants and even crop the heads off orchids!

The quarries have never been allowed to have land fill, something to do with their proximity to the water table and danger of pollution. They are private property but it would be nice if they could be purchased by the council for they would make a superb place for a natural history park and perhaps in Quarry III some swathes of artificial planting but of ecologically sympathetic species (Rubeckias, Echinops, Echiums etc).

Typical glade in Chalk Pit II.

'Cromer's Oak' from this photograph in winter it can be seen from its twisty branches that it is a hybrid. It has the stalked leaf and sessile acorn of Quercus petraea and the convoluted branch habit of Quercus robur.

One might assume that the quarries have frequent illegal visitors by the numbers of well worn paths ....but if one looks carefully it can be seen that these trails have been trampled and kept clear not by bi-peds, but by another species of four footed animal, the badger. To set a hide and film the early evening 'night life' would possibly make a interesting wildlife film. The biggest night time prowlers are the numerous badgers but there must be foxes as well that come down into the quarries from the surrounding woods. I have not noted any setts in the quarry itself but there may be some along the far northern side where there is more soil. (More about those on the next pages.)

Several quarries in Kent have been set aside for wildlife parks with public access and even if access was charged (which would be warranted) I feel certain it would be a valued and popular destination for week-end walks. At present the potential seems a little wasted (remember there are no public footpaths and one should ask permission to walk on private land).

Above the quarry, in the Highsted Wood itself there are several species of note and the most important (in my opinion) is a tree. It is far more unusual and of biological note than the numerous badgers. Someone keen to observe the badgers has, at some time, constructed a hide and has damaged one specimen of this unusual tree by affixing an angle iron to support this hide! The other specimen, close by, has survived damage in the severe 1987 hurricane and now seems to be recovering.

They are specimens of a variety of oak that many people probably do not realise is <u>different</u> from our now common oak here in the south. What is usually termed the "common" oak is **Quercus robur** and that has the familiar stalked acorn that looks like a clay pipe. The acorn of this other species has no stalk and its leaf has a longer stalk than that of Q.robur.

This second species of oak is **Quercus petraea** (more common in the west of England and Wales) is called a variety of names, the sessile oak, or durmast oak. That last name is curious as no one seems to know its derivation. Perhaps it was used for poles (masts) and because the wood was slightly different than common oak, more flexible and more heavily impregnated with tannin (redder in colour) the masts lasted a long time hence the name *'dura'*. (I mean land masts, ships often had pine masts but their rudders were of oak). It is noted that durmast oak has less 'figuring' (medullary rays) and is consequently sometimes confused with chestnut even by the experts! Here is an extract from L. J. F. Brimble *"Trees in Britain"* ....."*It is of interest to note that much of the wood in old buildings in the west of England, Wales and Ireland, formerly believed to be chestnut, is now known to be durmast oak: the same can be said of the carved roof in Westminster Hall. .... Since both these species of oak have reigned in Britain for many centuries, it should not be surprising that many hybrids (not yet described in detail) have arisen*".

Acorn of Quercus robur.

L. J. F. Brimble was somewhat of an expert on trees when he wrote his book in 1948 and still (as far as I know) no one has done a complete survey of these different types of oak.

"What does it matter?" I hear someone ask, not a lot I suppose, but it does give historical and archeological insight to various things. Rodmersham Church (just 1.5 miles distant) has a unique rood screen. It is possibly one of the only churches in the country that has a chestnut screen ...or so my expert cabinet maker father told me ......but I now think he made a mistake! Is it the same kind of wood as the roof of Westminster Hall? It would be highly unlikely that "holy oak" was substituted by chestnut. It is much more likely that the two specimens of durmast oak still growing in Highsted Wood were descendants of those that went to make the Rodmersham screen. In the wood of Oak Tree Farm (see the O.S. map in Chapter 1) in 1950, there were huge rotting boles of felled oaks. I have looked recently but they have at last all rotted away ....were they durmast oaks? All the oaks in that wood now are the common oak ***Quercus robur***.

The 'Cromer's Oak' .....*a hybrid of* Quercus petraea *(formerly Q. sessiflora) commonly called Sessile Oak, or Durmast Oak.*

Actual tree with fence damaged root base

Upper surface of leaf dark glossy green

Undersurfaces hairless light viridian green

Acorns stalkless

Researched by Lesley Feakes Aug. 1995

Right: 15th c. sedilia, drawn by Eric Goldsmith

Left: Photograph of the rood screen in Rodmersham Church.

One of the church wardens, Eric Goldsmith, is very knowledgeable on Rodmersham Church and together we had a close inspection of the screen. Certain sections **do** seem to be oak with the characteristic figuring of the medullary rays but other sections have none. The entire screen is the deep red colour of chestnut, darker sections appear to be older. In the church restoration in the 19th Century experts of the day (1881) diagnosed the wood as "chestnut"; that my father, independently, came to the same conclusion denotes that the screen is very unusual ....did those experts (including my father) make a mistake? Was most of the screen constructed of durmast heart wood that has few, if any, medullary rays and caused their confusion? Brimble's comment would imply that this is so ....anyone willing to solve the mystery can visit the church and work things out for themselves. Rodmersham also has a very fine example of a 15th century wooden sedilia and very few survived the reformation. The wood of this triple seated sedilia is the same colour as the screen but has plenty of areas with medullary rays, so is it again durmast oak?

Was the Bronze Age "Dover Boat" manufactured from a durmast oak? The size of the timbers suggests a **massive** tree and these oaks used to growing in wetter more acid soils (the climate was wetter then) would grow to huge heights (50metres or more). The largest oak tree in England is one growing in Herefordshire and it is a specimen of *Quercus petraea*. Trees I have looked at in Highwoods, Bexhill, Sussex - where there is a large stand, show great variety. One has a leaf size of 24 cm. (10 inches) and a huge acorn to match (3 cm. long)...but the tree itself has been coppiced about 100 years ago so is not that tall and has not reached its potential.

So imagine this scenario ...huge oaks bigger than you have ever seen growing, stand towering above the countryside ....does that give a better meaning to Highsted, Highstead, Higham, Great Higham* and High Woods? (For some of these places are not very 'high' geographically.) Are they remnants of the past areas where these kingly oaks were grown to provide timber, "holy oak" for the Bronze Age and Iron Age boats, and much much later for the Armada? Oaks were known as 'Holy' trees long before Christ was hung on one. Certain oaks have been held sacred by many Indo-Germanic people, perhaps an echo of that reverence can be felt in translations reputedly from the Book of the

* There are no trees now at Great Higham, but there are Q. petraea in Torry Hill Wood

Essenes about the huge sacred trees.

Perhaps trees sacred to the god Thor can be explained by scientific facts ...lightning strikes oak trees more than any other species and it is not because they are taller, because in modern times when that statistic was established many trees equal their height. But it is maybe something to do with their water transport and natural electrical charge, who knows until it is studied.

One tree that shows the typical tall trunk and terminal fan of branches that is not like the broad spreading habit of most 'common' oaks in Kent today, is this one in a wood near Milstead. It has the stalked leaf of *Q.petraea* also and the sessile (stalkless) acorn. Sometimes the features are separated and not all hybrids are so true to type. It is quite likely that these examples of the older form are remnants of populations that clothed Iron Age sites. This area of Milstead is indeed yielding clues to its ancient past with Iron Age and Roman finds. Perhaps if people did more research and observation to confirm that the species-type and prehistoric sites do link, my theory would be proven.

The 'Squires Walking Stick' An oak growing on Lord Longford's estate, Co. W. Meath, Ireland, has most of the Quercus Petraea features. 12.5m to the first branches.

Mistletoe reputedly grew on oaks, I have never seen it on one in Kent for it is usually on Limes (eg. Sutton Vallence, Linton, Chilham) and on apple along the spring line of the Weald. At Woodstock it is on field maple, as one can see in the photo over the page. The legend that the Mistletoe was sacred and was gathered by the Druids, is likely true. Is it possible that it grew on the durmast oaks, rather than our now commoner species of English oak? I think that is most likely so. As I say, I have yet to see it growing on a modern oak in Kent (can anyone tell me if it does?)

Quarter stater (x 2)

This durmast oak in Marley Wood near Kingston, Kent, has an enormous side arm. It is possible this feature is genetically controlled and its ancestors had a similar growth habit. If that is true then it gives meaning to the depiction of an oak with apparent long side arm that is found on this? stater gold Celtic type "D" coin found nearby! Did the local oaks and those in N.France, where the same coin series is found, have similar phenotypes?

In the Weald, where mistletoe is more common, the oaks seem to be a stumpy variety with a very 'frilly' very indentated *Q.robur* leaf, but no mistletoe in evidence. They have no shortage of water but do not seem to achieve the massive height of durmast oaks. In conversation with one friend she came out with the comment :-

"Growth of mistletoe is allied to the electricity of the tree." .... I have thought about her spontaneous words very carefully ....perhaps she is right!

Mistletoe has an unusual growth pattern, it branches dichotomously i.e. divides like a genealogical family tree in an even pattern. Perhaps ancients could see a similarity in Man and God ....follow the branches back far enough and one reaches the source, the sustinance ....the root = God.

Mistletoe is a very curious plant. It is a monocotyledon and has distinctive parallel veins to the leaf. It is parasitic but is dependent on the host tree's water supply (xylem) more than its phloem vessels (those carrying the sugary sap) for the plant is green all over and that indicates it has some chlorophyll and can synthesise its own sugars. The stickiness of its berries makes sure that they adhere to birds bills and are carried to other trees for the seeds to grow there.

Woodstock Field Maple - with Mistletoe

Mistletoe - with its sticky white berries, even dichotamous branching and greenish yellow leaves and stems.

Highsted Wood when the coppicing shows off the bluebells and the lower part of the 'Hollow Way' as it curves around the site.

The Highsted Wood is very wet, the rain water puddling on the clay soil. When it was coppiced in recent years the whole woodland floor was carpeted with germinating rushes, both the common soft rush *Juncus effusus* and the toad rush, *Juncus bufonius*. Both are quite common, but both indicate a damp soil.

In the spring the whole wood is carpeted with bluebells and the lower section around the area of the boundary stone is swathed with wild garlic or ramsons.

Boundaries of woods are often ditched and banked. The question would be with Highsted Wood whether the boundary was made on an existing bank which was kept as the limits to the woodland. It is possible that this is so, and along the higher inside bank of the 'hollow way' is a very ancient row of coppiced hornbeams. They have been allowed to grow unchecked in recent years and are losing their stumpiness of the typical stooled hornbeam ....but they are very old. One ash stool also is of great age.

Some of the chestnut stools are 3 metres across and some look as if they were once a single stool but now are a ring of smaller stools that have become separate as the centre dies and has rotted away.

One of the ancient hornbeams:
The trunk of the durmast oak is behind it to the right.

Field Maple:- Standing in the corner of the wood is a massive field maple. It again is of a great age and one of the largest that most people have ever seen in Kent. I have recently noted another at Thurnham Castle, and as that is now being 'put on the map' as a public Trust area, it is worth walking up to see that one (and the spectacular view).

Field maples were always kept in the hedgerows as 'marker' trees. I was pleased to note that the house I have just bought although new, has had a maple hedge planted at the front ....the old boundary markers are coming back in popularity! In the autumn its leaves go a very pleasing butter yellow.

Green Woodpecker or yaffle :-this is perhaps one of our commonest woodpeckers but I have included it here because so many people working on site in 1996 and 1998 commented on it. It was as though it were laughing at us all scrabbling around in the dirt, and it invariably gave us a cocky fly-past every time we were there, yaffling its head off! Old cherry trees suit it very much for nest sites and it usually drills the hole about at head height. It is a very colourful bird indeed.

Although there seemed to be few birds around in the hot summer months we were there, during autumn and spring there are a great many of the common varieties. When on the site after a rainy spell it is noticeable that the bird song from the quarry wafts up like a dawn chorus.

It is possible that the numerous badgers in the wood deter blackbirds and thrushes from nesting in the woodland and they have moved down into the quarry for safer homes. Badgers are omnivores and are quite partial to eggs, so I suspect that the thrush family (notoriously careless nesters, choosing such obvious sites) have got wiped out in the wood.

Butterflies and moths:

Although we did not notice any of the rarer species of butterfly, the quantity was remarked on so often by different people. In an area such as the grassy edge to the Highsted quarry where there has been no fruit tree spraying, the common species of butterfly are able to build up numbers. One Lepidopteran that shouts out its presence by its flamboyant colouring is the six spot burnet moth. Two can be seen on the photograph of rose-bay willow herb. Their red markings often show a great variation, the spots sometimes merging. The background of the wing is black, but it gleams in an iridescent glow of greenish-

Cinnabar moth and caterpillar.

blue. The noticeable colouring is to proclaim the fact that these moths are poisonous, containing molecules of cyanide. They feed on the bird's foot trefoil, *Lotus corniculatus* that is very common in the area. Another poisonous moth joins forces with the burnet moth, the cinnabar moth, *Tyria jacobaeaea*, feeds on ragwort and is a similar bright red and black. It can be distinguished by its red stripe along the top of the wing. Two species with similar warning colourations mutually benefit from each other, birds soon get to know their advertising colours and leave both well alone. Cinnabar caterpillars are also distasteful to birds and display the well known black and orange 'football jersey 'stripes. Ragwort contains a mercuric alkaloid poison and is the reason why it is so poisonous to mammals. The sheep leave it well alone! I have painted a picture of that moth, (and its caterpillar) note the difference in the red and black markings from the six spot burnet.

Other butterflies:- seen in the area,

Small skipper, small white, large white, wall, small tortoiseshell, comma, painted lady, red admiral, peacock, gate keeper, meadow brown, speckled wood, brimstone, common blue, adonis blue, and there maybe many more. But there do not seem to be any of the fritillaries.

Badgers:- I have left this species to last. Their tracks all over the area give clues to their presence. Over the last ten years or so their numbers have increased and my rough count last summer was 14 openings to setts. Highsted is not the only piece of woodland in the area that is their home and as their numbers appear to be rising and they are very territorial, pressure of real estate for badgers must mean that they will gradually spread to other suitable woods .

However, their presence at Highsted is almost inevitable from two counts.

1. They like the sandy soil (although much is clay there seems to be a section of Thanet Sands)

2. It is known that badgers often sett over 'blind springs'. These are springs that are beneath the ground and only in exceptional wet weather do they surface. Blind springs also seem to be under western gates of ancient settlement sites! Not suprisingly, the area of the setts is in the likely area of the west gate.

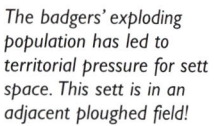

Rosebay willowherb and a pair of six spot burnet moths.

The badgers' exploding population has led to territorial pressure for sett space. This sett is in an adjacent ploughed field!

Chapter 10

"Into the Fringe"

In this chapter I will try and explain certain facts that show that the "fringe" of accepted archaeology expands as more becomes known. Its like approaching a rainbow, more and more scientific knowledge is gained but the full understanding still remains ahead of us. Static electricity and magnetism are two aspects of science that previously had a 'mystique' attached to them; they still do in some people's eyes.

> "And time can crumble all but cannot touch
> The book that burns faster than one can read"
>
> Michael Roberts

Working with the Van der Graaf Generator.

If this photograph were shown to someone who lived some 300 years ago they would likely have said it was the work of "witches"! Even some modern people might be surprised by the effects of static electricity. But modern science pupils familiar with the Van der Graaf generator would excitedly explain to you what is happening and why.

Unfortunately the study of electricity has now been withdrawn from the National Curriculum in schools in England, which is a great pity. Use of the Van der Graaf generator (no danger of *any* dangerous shocks) gave an informative and very interesting lesson to introduce children to the somewhat amazing aspects of static electricity. The longer a child's hair the more spectacular the effect! When one is charged up in this way water will respond to the charge and seemingly bend towards ones finger defying gravity!

Laboratory taps have a thin stream of water flowing from them and this is ideal to show the effect of the static charge.

Sometimes it will move even as far as 45° from the vertical stream **against** the force of gravity, the second photograph shows that.

A girl in one of my lessons packed an amazing charge. After being on the Van der Graaf generator, she managed to discharge a shock to 20 pupils before her body charge returned to normal (the usual was about 3 discharges.)

A facsimile of a child's description of what happens.

Miss made me stand on a plastic tray and switched on the ball thing. A belt moved round it and the friction energy changed into static electricity and my hair began to crackle. I could not feel anything but my hair felt funny When I put my finger towards Staceys a spark cracked across like lectric litening. Miss said it was because the electrisity had not run to earth but it ran down through Stacey. She squealed because it made her jump. The thing was called a a Van der Graaf generator.

My drawing

But in another class I noted that one red-headed boy said he was *'No good'* on the generator, he never built up a charge at all, or if he did, then it was not discharging again and he was somehow just absorbing the static!

Here of course, is a demonstrable scientific explanation of how water dowsing does in fact work. The electro-static charge of the water is attracted to the charge in ones body. Instead of the water 'bending', as it does from this tap, the hazel twig or the metal rods will sway or move down towards the water. As in the case described in Chapter 6, the dowser will be aware of the force and sometimes the rods or the hazel twig will spring out of their hands.

"Oh, but people claim they can dowse stone walls!" I hear the sceptics chant. Yes, that is possible because stone often retains a film of water when the surrounding soil is bone dry. This differential in electrostatic charge is again detectable using dowsing rods. Now, in year 2001, after recent torrential rains I would suspect that definitive dowsing becomes very difficult, for the water is everywhere!

But it seems evident from my school experiments that the sensitivity to static charges varies in different people and I would think it highly likely that some people are affected more than others by magnetism also. Electricity, magnetism, light are all different forms of the **same thing**. Faraday showed us that, and our modern light lasers are electricity travelling through a magnetic

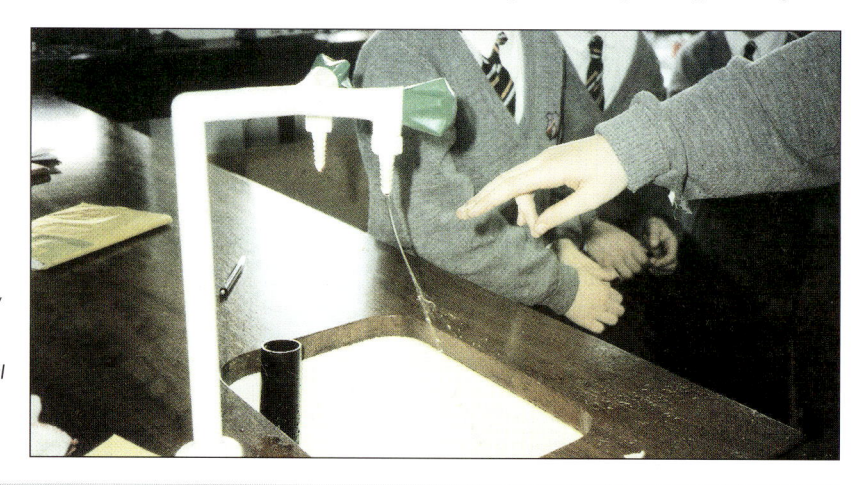

*Laboratory taps have a thin stream of water flowing from them and this is ideal to show the effect of the static charge Sometimes it will move even as far as 45° from the vertical stream **against** the force of gravity, the photograph shows that:-*

field. We can see light ...is it not possible that some people can feel magnetism? We can feel electricity ...at what point and strength does that electricity become so magnetic that we cannot escape from it?

Some people can dowse just using their hands and some people can mentally sense 'vibes' as to what is under the ground. So how are they doing it? Where does one draw a line in saying that is possible and that is nonsense? Let me stretch some peoples acceptance of the limit they believed possible .....a little further into that fringe ....

In one lesson about magnetism two boys were obviously engrossed in something on their own. When I went to see what they were doing it was clear they were having a 'competition' to see if they could force two horseshoe magnets together the wrong way around (with like poles opposite). One of the lads in particular was totally fascinated by the power he could feel. " *Do you think you could feel that power with just one of them?*" I asked him. "*Of course not!*" the other said emphatically. But it was an ideal opportunity to encourage them to invent their own experiment.

Experiments are part of the National Curriculum in Science; pupils have to be able to devise experiments that present a fair test, write up the experiment making sure that it tests the theory and controls the variables. The task I set them was to invent an experiment to test whether some people can detect magnetism. They were allowed to use strong horseshoe magnets, polystyrene cups and blindfolds. The best experiment, devised by one pupil, controlled all the variables, yet repeatedly this particular girl found the magnet 100% of the time. They could not catch her out! Everyone else seemed to be guessing with a chance 50:50 success rate; afterwards I asked her how she did it.

She explained that she could feel a slight 'buzzing' through her finger-tips around the cup with the magnet concealed beneath. As she had been out of the room when they were set and there was no cheating going on, I have no reason to doubt her. She could detect the magnet, through nerves in her finger tips ...she could tell where it was. Let us take this concept further.

It is scientific fact, now proven by medical research, that our brains respond to incoming electro-magnetic currents. Certain parts of the cerebral hemispheres respond to different frequencies and thoughts and emotions of fear, happiness, euphoria and even 'spiritual encounters' can be artificially induced. So, if certain areas of the Earth have higher levels of electro-magnetic radiation do some sensitive people respond to them in having 'induced' thoughts, inspirational brain waves? Does a source of water with a high static charge affect people? Evidence suggests that it does.

Another known and proven fact .....if there has been human activity in a certain area the surrounding soil becomes more magnetic and the difference can be detected by using a magnetometer (see the geophysical investigation Chapter 6). Working with Alister Bartlett on a later occasion I was recording magnetism on a field in Harrietsham, Kent. There was a distinct rectangular area of slightly higher magnetism in the centre of the field ....not a hidden ancient building, it was the cricket table! The increased human activity, mowing, rolling, playing cricket, had left its mark!

Now, if I were a medium, which I am not, or someone supersensitive to magnetism I could presumably have mentally detected the magnetism/ previous human activity on that area without using an instrument!

Is that statement I have just made totally unacceptable to previous sceptics? Or have I managed to stretch your preconceived limits of thought into the fringe? Where does the fringe drop down a limiting curtain? Or is it just that we have not allowed our brains to accept that there are realms of particle physics that we still do not fully understand and because we do not understand them we tend to let our 'logic' say that they do not exist!

Apparently American archaeologists have used mediums on ancient Amerind sites for years and with considerable success. When are British archaeologists going to drop their intolerance and realise that such people have a valid place in serious investigations? There are certain facts that **cannot** be determined from artefacts and classic investigations alone. It is my suspicion that ancient (and also not so old) sites somehow leave an 'echo' of past events ...exactly how this happens we do not know as yet ...but the answer will lie in particle physics I feel sure. Somehow that 'echo' plays back through people's minds. Einstein's theory is still a theory ...we have not proven that "Time is relative to the speed we are travelling at"...maybe when we prove he is right then we will also understand 'ghosts' and 'time warps'.

I was married to a Hindu and two of our Hindu friends (mirror image identical twins) explained the higher points of Hinduism to me. One brother had a Ph.D. in particle physics and the other a Ph.D. in physical chemistry and as they were Brahmins (priest caste) they were very knowledgeable. They explained that there are aspects of particle physics that are way beyond our comprehension, there is so much still to discover. Within the science of physics they allowed for an extension ...metaphysics, that stretches way past our present knowledge into the realm of God. The Hindu belief in many 'gods' is only relative, relative to one's brain capacity ....God is so immense that it is impossible for us to hold the whole ....so for most Hindus it is acceptable to fragment Him/Her into several smaller pieces ....but it does not detract from the concept there is only one Godhead. However, many Hindus pay deference to Shiva, the God of destruction and the recent findings on 'black holes' makes us realise that indeed there are two opposing energies, equivalent to creation and destruction! Hinduism is hugely complex or is very simple, one only has to believe one thing e.g. there is only one Godhead ...and one is a Hindu. One brother also explained to me that it is their belief that civilisation has not progressed in a smooth curve. It is possible that there was a peak of civilisation way back in the past (beyond 5000 years if not twice that) and we have gone backwards in some respects, knowledge has been lost! For example, it is written in the Vedas (over 5000 yrs ago) that the Lord Vishnu came on his 'Vimanas' and that is only translatable by the words :- 'flying-machine'.

No, one does **not** have to start believing in extra-terrestrials ...Man has had the materials to make hot air balloons for centuries ....it is just the technical know-how that was needed. I will add here again (if I have not said it before) I use 'Man' as the name for mankind that 'man' is also the name of a male of the species is immaterial.

One can also philosophize this way: if Man of the future cracks the time barrier, to travel backwards in time to their past ...we would have to see their space machines in our present! So how do we know UFO,s are not time machines of our future? Could they be using lines of limitless energy ...the Earth's magnetic field? So why should anyone scoff at the comment that 'ley' lines are 'paths' for UFO's? If one is truly a scientist one has to keep an open mind it *could* be a correct statement!

Is it an insular tendency of English people to think that we are the 'best', that methods of British archaeology are the 'best' and that people who extend into the fringe realms are 'nutters'? I will broach another subject that few archaeologists in Britain seem to wish to expand on, that of the 'Atlantis' theory. Many legends imply that there was such a place ....so why should it not have been so? Also, archaeology needs to keep apace of the people; without doubt there are many of us who have had some kind of metaphysical/spiritual experience at some time in our lives, yet so many archaeologists talk of 'ritual' archaeology and spirituality as if it is something alien to their actual experience, as if they believe scientists should not believe such things actually exist! Isn't it about time that we say to sceptics who scoff and jeer... *"Why are you so afraid of a phenomenon that is part and parcel of archaeology?"* Spirituality exists, whether we prefer to explain it in electro-magnetic terms, or more profound ones **it does exist.**

It is part of ancient archaeology and it is part of the present.

Two cats I have owned in the past few years have been able to discharge an electrical current at will. No, it was **not** my imagination! The neutered ginger Tom I had at Bexhill just did not like being picked up as he grew older. He would show his displeasure by discharging a shock down my hand and arm and I would promptly drop him! The current seemed to come from his thorax area and I have noticed that when toms are furious and about to fight another cat their hackles crackle with static electricity! Why more study has not been done on this ability of cats I do not know. As a zoologist this generating of a an electrical charge in a mammal greatly intrigues me. When my daughter came home one week-end she picked up the cat then promptly dropped him in disbelief!..... *"He gave me a shock!"* she yelled. *"Sorry, I had not told you because I thought you would not believe me!"* I said. We then had a scientific discussion as to how a mammal might be generating a charge rather like an electric eel!

The Egyptians classed cats as 'gods', so was this the reason that they did? Did they know more about electricity that we realize ....on certain nights of the year the Bedouins will tell you that there is a flame glowing on the apex of the Great Pyramid!

What knowledge was lost in the great library of Alexandria when it was burned by the Caliph of Baghdad? How many of those books would have burnt our minds with their 'advanced' information?

CELTIC KNOWLEDGE of MAGNETISM:-

It is quite likely, in my estimation, that Bronze (and/or Neolithic) Age Celts could use the magnetism of the Earth to set the lines of the reaves. Either they had an innate response to the magnetic field or they used a form of compass. The latter is the most acceptable theory to most people, no doubt, but even so some might disbelieve that this is possible. I assure you it is! Again, teaching magnetism in school it is a standard experiment to make a simple compass by floating a magnetized needle on the surface tension of a water in a petri dish. It works very well! Bronze Age peoples would not have had magnetic iron but would have had magnetite (the magnetic ore) that would work just as well ....a sliver floating on a bowl of water. Using a compass seems the logical method of sighting the lines because using the stars would not be possible in the daylight.

It is a possibility that the reaves of Devon and the parallel SW→NE trackways of Kent were all set at the same time for they run in the same direction. It is not without possibility that at that time magnetic north was way off beam and was some 20 degrees east of grid north and therefore they were set on that archaeic line of magnetic north. Later (or earlier) the Half-mile path near Sittingbourne may have been set on a re-alignment.......... And so to Chapter 11.........

P.S.
On the evening I completed this chapter I had dinner with my art group at the Black Horse, Pluckley. Pluckley strides the Wychling line and other people have noted other alignments too...... it is reputedly the most haunted village in Kent (if not England!) Inevitably we got talking about ghosts. A friend told of her 'haunted' house in the village (closer to the Wychling line than the pub) then she remarked in the next sentence that she had just had to dig a ditch around the house because it was so wet!

So with the 'explanations' I have given in this chapter several concepts switch in to explain Pluckleys 'ghosts'.
1. Underground water — giving a high electro-static charge
2. Ancient route ways through the village could have increased the magnetism
3. Pluckley could have a naturally high electro-magnetic field.
All might trigger peoples brain activity and /or cause replay of events as 'ghosts'.

77

Kit's Coty

Reflections on Kipling's 'Neolithic Age'

When a poet writes his lines
Within them can he hide the truth.
Not so with prose I think you'll find
Where scoffs and jeers can hurt and kill…
Can kill good thought and put our knowledge back apace
Not openly reveal…
The ways our ancestors did live and love, communicate and feel.
That knowledge deep within our past and soul
Can surface and tell us all,
Can flood like water in the pool
Of Life, with Peace …and cool.

'Tis not the lings that hold the power
But our minds that tank the Peace
Then our Love can grow and flower
Down mental highways wars to cease!

The truth is clear, it does not veil
If one floats above the pale…
One sees the mystic realms of Christ.
Kipling used the leys…to discover Neolithic ways
Then told us in a poetry of mist.

The mists of time confused the sign
Earth's power became a 'sin'.
'Tis not true the Weald had few…
People living in its Bronze Age past…
'Twas only Saxon myth and fear that lost the ways in forest mast!

But Baptists came with spirit bold, just like Old.
Built their Wealden Houses square across the line.
Did they not know? That God's true flow
Is Earth and Water, Spirit free, that gives the Life to you and me…
God's blood and wine .

Christ! The Dodman of the Downs revealed.
His ways are straight His heart still true. He communicates to me and you
Through the Universal Love and plight
You may think my lines are long, may rant and rave… I've got it wrong!
(But remember what the bard did say afore ……)
There are nine and sixty ways of understanding ancient leys
And-every-single-one-of-them-is-right!

Lesley Feakes 23-12-2000

Chapter 11

"The People who Walked Straight"

The title of this chapter comes from a saying referring to north American and Central American Indians who were said, and say of themselves that they are the "People who Walk Straight". I first heard the expression from a Canadian when I was living in Canada. He told me that the Mohawks earned very good money in Toronto on sky-scraper construction sites. Apparently they walk with their feet one in front of the other and can therefore walk straighter than we do and not lose their balance on the high steel girders. But that is not the whole story – there are many accounts of the Indians being able to track for miles and miles in a remarkably straight line. The record of these straight lines is perhaps shown very enigmatically on the plains of Nazca in S. America. The Nazca lines have been man-made by scoring the surface soil deposits to expose the different colour underneath.

> *"But my totem saw the shame; from his ridge-pole shrine he came,*
> *And he told me of a vision of the night:-*
> *There are nine and sixty ways of constructing tribal lays*
> *And every single one of them is right!"*
> Rudyard Kipling
> 'In the Neolithic Age'

Did many Neolithic people have the genetic ability to walk a straight line (deviating only where there was a natural hazard) and have an exceptional perception of space and orientation, where they were on the Earth's surface? Did this ability have a spiritual significance to them? The references to John the Baptist and his walking straight lines in the desert may not just have been metaphorical! If there is something in this concept of straight line thought then the reaves and trackways of Kent are an important contribution to the understanding of this ancient tradition.

The 'Half Mile Path' near Sittingbourne is under threat of being destroyed forever ….there is a proposed housing development across it. It is possible the track was disrupted when brick earth was removed to either side of it in the 19th century **but** it was kept in the same alignment, and for all we know could once have been a hollow way (the banks now sliced off). Bronze Age and Roman funeral urns were found on both sides of that trackway. It is a great pity that the one trackway that might be proof of the ancient system is due to be destroyed and no one seems to care!

Some urns found in the lower end of Highsted School playing fields, (my secondary school) were smashed up by the workmen who discovered them in the 19th century! The disregard for ancient finds has a history in the area; a Roman lead coffin found in the 19th century was melted down to mend the gas pipes of Sittingbourne!

I have broached the theory before that Neolithic people could detect the Earth's magnetism. Many Amerind people walked in bare feet and a TV programme about a 'lost' tribe in Venuzuela mentioned how important it was to them to feel 'Mother Earth' through contact with their feet! *"Take off thy shoes from off thy feet"* may have had a scientific truth, for where would one feel the Earth's magnetism …..but through ones feet!

The 'Half Mile Path' is set on magnetic north!

It is a possibility that the reave system of Devon and the parallel SW→NE trackways system of Kent (and across into Sussex) were both set at the same time. It is not without possibility that at that time magnetic north was way off beam and was some 20 degrees east of grid north and therefore they were set on that archaic position of magnetic north. It is conjecture whether the 'setters' were sensing the magnetic direction by an innate ability or using a simple compass as suggested in the previous chapter.

Is there a strong connection between the Neolithic peoples of the Americas and those of Britain and Western Europe? Genetic fingerprinting is beginning to point to the fact that many peoples are closer genetically than we once thought. Have traditions remained as 'markers' also? Neolithic people in Britain built longhouses and practised excarnation of the dead (placing their dead on platforms to be picked clean by the birds of the air before burial) similar to some N. American tribes.

Here are photographs of that path near Sittingbourne. If you look carefully at the bottom picture it is possible to see that the trackway follows magnetic north as it is today. This suggests that it was set in an age when magnetic north was in the same alignment as now. (Remember it wobbles and is now some 5 west of true north.)

I have included totem poles in my reconstruction drawings and strangely, my inclination to do that <u>preceded</u> my knowledge that archaeologists now think that wooden totem poles were part of the Neolithic and Bronze Age scene.

The Woodstock tumulus (described in the last chapter), the Binbury motte on Detling, and Thurnham motte were all similar and reinforced with flints. It is clear when viewing Binbury (and that motte ought to be honoured and cared for as an ancient monument) that flint must be maintaining the gradient else it would have slumped far more than it has. On Thurnham it is obvious this is the case, and the flints form and maintain the steep banks. Dane John at Canterbury is another 'pudding basin' type mound that has a similar gradient and height. Lewes, in Sussex, has several such mounds; whether they are all prehistoric is debatable, but they could be!

If there were huge wooden masts set on these mounds, then they would have needed a large hole and a hard-core support of flints or stones. Woodstock and Thurnham both had/have depressions in the top. These may have been caused by 'grave robbers', or from flint robbing <u>or</u> from the presence of a large post-hole!

Looking up the 'Half Mile Path' towards the North.

Trackway with a compass

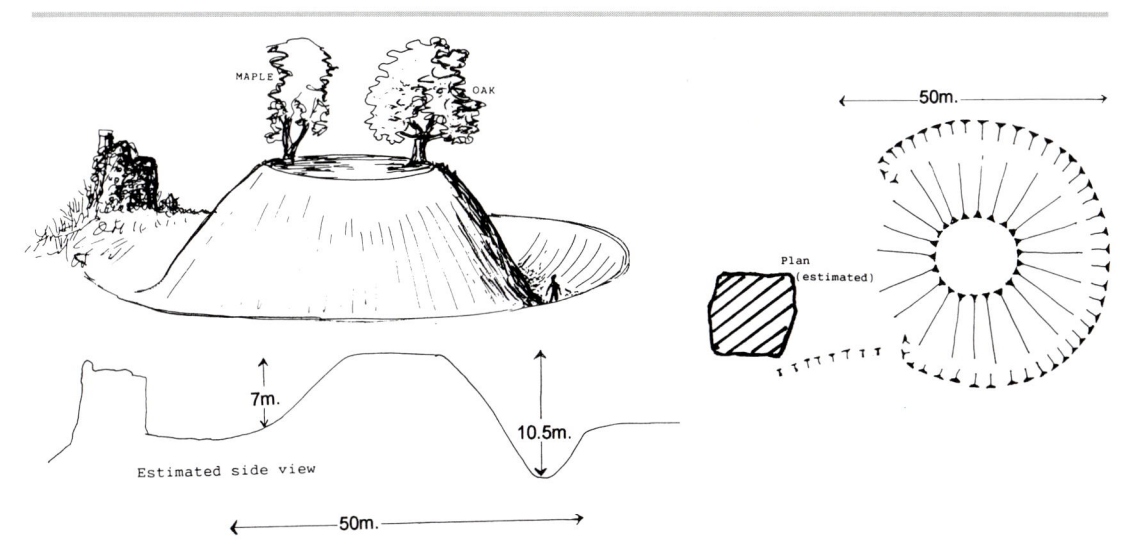

Binbury motte and Thurnham lie roughly north-south of each other. If someone were on top of a pole or tower on both, visual contact could be maintained between the two.

Binbury commands a view as far as Essex and Herne Bay (on the coast of Kent). Thurnham views 180° south right across the Weald as far as Fairlight near Hastings on the Sussex coast, and from Hythe to Sevenoaks and Oldbury. Smoke signals would be an easy proposition between the various points .

It is possible Binbury and Thurnham were set N→S of each other on a magnetic reading when magnetic north was some 5 east of grid north. Is there any connection between the Kentish mounds and the mounds on the Essex marshes near Barling? These are all questions that spring to mind and questions that could be looked into. Scoffers who have for years shouted down the importance of alignments in the ancient British landscape have delayed the investigation of these ancient possibilities. The fact that both Binbury and Thurnham have adjacent flint walls, medieval 'castles,' does not deflect from the possibility the sites are far, far older.

When I looked at the banking system plan I had drawn of Woodstock, several years ago, I was struck by the navicular shape of the site. It was like a huge boat with a square northern 'stern' and rounded 'prow' sailing due south west. So why did it sail in that direction? I drew the S.W. line without looking at any points on the map, just drew it right across the chart, even through France.

Then I looked at the points on the line.

It hit the Quiberon peninsular and Carnac on the west coast of Britany. It crossed the English coast through Seaford Head (ancient site) and it was aligned by the barrow on Windover Hill atop the Long Man of Wilmington! Going N.E. up the line it went through Batemans ….and I laughed because that was Rudyard Kipling's house! He was a freemason and well into ancient thought and ancient enigmas as I point out again in the next chapter!

He wrote :-

> "I will go out against the Sun
> Where the rolled scarp retires
> And the Long Man of Wilmington
> Looks naked toward the Shires."

BINBURY mound near Detling, Kent. Twice the size of Woodstock Mound, but similar in description.

Note:- August 2001. A news bulletin has just shown Silbury Hill, Wiltshire. It has developed a hole in its top and helicopters were being used to haul loads of flint/chalk/soil to fill it in. So my query continues, did it once support a mast? Silbury with a 40m. tree mast would be a truly impressive sight, visible for miles!

My 1997 acrylic painting of Windover Hill, Sussex

I expect many people realise that Carnac in Britany is a very important Neolithic centre. *"Les Alignements"* stretch out in rows and rows many of the lines pointing in a N.E. direction …..back to Woodstock and Kent?

Checking the line still further I realised it went through Glassenbury and Hawkenbury in the Weald of Kent and through a moated site Moatenden. That site had long intrigued me as it was reputedly a Trinitarian monks' site and formerly a 12th century manor house, but the report in *Arch. Cant. 115.* 1995

"Les Alignements" at Carnac, Brittany, (painting, 1998)

82

says some Romano-British grog tempered pottery was found *'beneath the cloister garth soils'*.

Remembering that the reave lines are Neolithic/Bronze Age, and run parallel to this line I am now considering ….is it too impertinent to query whether the 'medieval moated site' was built atop a Romano-British one, atop a Bronze Age one, and below that, Neolithic site? To say I am chasing 'make believe' lines in the landscape is not valid, it is illogical to say they are definitely <u>not</u> there when the directions I have followed indicate they definitely <u>could</u> be.

What was under Fishbourne Roman Palace? Would it be valid to excavate one of its beautiful mosaics just to see if the Roman site was atop an Iron Age/Bronze Age even Neolithic site? ……possibly not, it would destroy too much! But the theory the Palace is standing on an older site is not new.

"Lings":- throughout my research for this book I have used J. Wallenberg's place name book, but place name investigators are not always right. The skill is often addicted to guess work. I have noticed that the *'ling'* and *'ing'* words in Kent are not necessarily attributable to 'inglas' which is Anglo-Saxon for *'people of'*.

Detling, Lidsing, Wychling and Eastling are all regions with high plateaux on the Downs. The Scottish word *'ling'* has two meanings, the plant that is related to heather and grows on moors, and the word meaning a *'line'*.

Wychling has a line. Detling has a possible line and Eastling is very peculiar as we shall see later. After I mentioned this to a friend she asked *'What about Postling?'*

I had to look for that one on the map as I did not know it, it is near Hythe. Immediately north of the village is a marked hill, north of that is a distinct wents in Sibton Wood and south of the village is Postling Wents. The line of those three co-ordinates points directly to a mound near Saltwood …in fact there are suitable hills in lines all around that area! So is my brainwave on 'post lines' fantasy or does the village of Postling give a clear answer? Surely it is worthy of research and more serious thought?

Wychling according to Wallenberg has a root meaning of *Wincel.* When I read that I was amazed for the name for Winchelsea was also *Wincel.* Why did I whistle? Because the Old town of Winchelsea was finally washed away by the great storm of 1287. They then built the new town where it is today, nobody knows the exact site of Old Winchelsea ….but I realised that the *'Wincel line'* might give the position. I had long thought that for Winchelsea to operate as a port it must have been on a spit of land originally attached to the mainland near Hastings. A headland would also have protected Rye and the waterways to Tenterden from silting up. After the spit was finally breached by the sea, and Winchelsea lost forever, the shingle from Beachy Head and beyond was free to move along the coast.

That is exactly what it started to do and the shingle bands built up in the last 1000 years can be seen quite distinctly on an 1920 aerial photograph.

The shingle had probably started to shift before the great storm of 1287, but when the Winchelsea spit had entirely gone it was free to build up to where it is now.

As the Dungeness headland grew, currents in the Rye bay changed and instead of the sea scouring out the mud, the bay silted up and Romney marsh extended.

Now, off Dungeness, the sea plunges to ten fathoms and more. This ten-fathom line is where the spit of Old Winchelsea probably extended out to (level with Dungeness point).

Vertical Plan of shingle banks of Dungeness
Sketched from a 1920 oblique aerial photograph.

The shingle had started to form by 1000A.D. One can assume that Winchelsea spit had already started to erode and the chalk stack at White Rock, Hastings was washing away.
In 1278 the complete annihilation of Old Winchelsea left the way open for movement of shingle from as far away as Beachy Head. Even now the coast is changing and the shore near Dungeness power stations is seriously eroding as the hook tends to drift N.E.

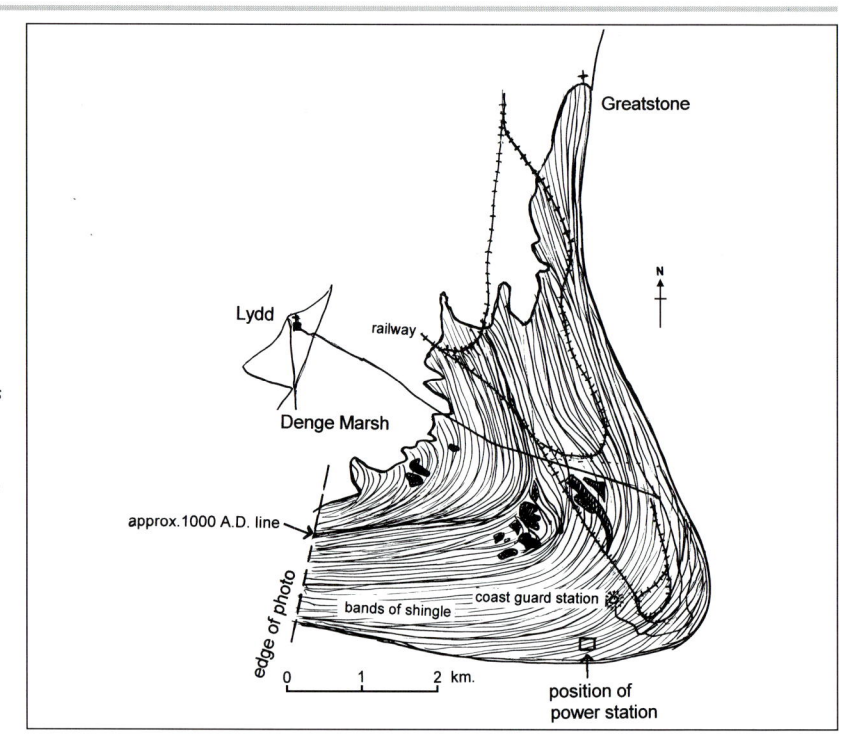

SO, if one sails out about $3^1/_2$ miles from Rye Harbour, takes a bearing on the northern alignment of St. Mary's Oxney with Bethersden's St.Margaret's and drops anchor, one should be within 100metres of the position of the bell-tower of Old Winchelsea Church. It is possible that Tower Knoll and Boulder Bank, underwater features on the Marine map, are remnants of that Winchelsea peninsular. Samuel Jeakes of Rye (17th Century) tells us that Winchelsea was said to have been a city in the time of the Romans.

'But you have lined medieval points' I hear someone shout! **No I have not** – I have used a very old Neolithic sighting line, the Wychling or Wincel line, and because churches were often sited on these very ancient lines I have predicted where Marine Archaeologists could start looking for Old Winchelsea! It is possible that when the line was originally set there was a land bridge and the English Channel did not exist at all at that point!

The *'People who Walked Straight'*, Neolithic people, might have set the line when they walked from France to England and back. In the museum of *Hougue Bie*, the large passage tomb in Jersey, there is a flint that is so like one we found at Woodstock it could be its twin, trade across the Channel area was commonplace in Neolithic times .

One last story about lines in the landscape: the antiquarians of the 19th century tell us that across the Medway valley between Coldrum Long Barrow at Trottiscliffe (pronounced Trosley) and Kits Coty House was an avenue of stones. It backs my theory that prehistoric people were very aware of compass directions. Thomas Wright F.S.A. writes in *'The Gentleman's Magazine'* of 1852:

"…it is the tradition of the peasantry that a continual line of such stones ran from Coldrum direct along the valley to the hill of Kit's Coty House, a distance of between five and six miles. Mr.Larkin and myself traced these stones in the line through a great portion of the distance, and their existence probably gave rise to the tradition."

Now, Coldrum Barrow faces out in a due east direction and Kit's Coty faces due west. That line would make a parallel one to the east→west 'church' line I described in the 'Trackway' chapter. *Except* this line is closer to true east→west …the other was fixed by magnetic north, and this one is 3.4km further north. but was this second E→W line set when magnetic North was in a different position?

It is difficult to give an accurate representation of that amazing avenue of stones because it was some six miles long, but I have attempted to draw it using some artistic licence and foreshortening. Perhaps both barrows were covered in chalk (as was Julliberie's Grave, near Canterbury) for that would make them more visible across the distance. Perhaps they were originally involved in a night time ceremony and the full moon would illuminate the massive stones (as the Antiquarians tell us they were *"colossal"*).

COLDRUM LONG BARROW
—*Trottiscliffe-looking due east to Kit's Coty*

Bronze Age Sarsen Avenue
- from Coldrum due east to Kit's Coty.
Note that artistic licence was necessary to forshorten the distance ...else the effect would be very difficult to portray.

Chapter 12

Beyond the Pale

If you examine my reconstruction of Woodstock on the cover, you will notice that there are black and white sculptures on the fencing pales. These naturally occurring flint nodules are often bizarre shapes and resemble animals sculptured by the Cretaceous seas. This ability to see animals within the natural shapes of nature, seem to be, a relic of our Celtic past. Some people with a less imaginative mind do not seem to appreciate these subtle art forms. My father found one of these on the farm (just across the valley from Woodstock) and he always called it his 'Henry Moore' sculpture. The second one featured here was found in the Highsted quarry and the third was found on site in the 1998 dig. Presumably the back of the 'Birds head' was humanly carved in prehistory.

Taking this pictorial 'nonsense' a stage further and to a much larger scale:

Did you notice Sheppey on my 'Trackway' map? My pencil has doodled in the high ground to look like an eye orbit and Harty has grown

Flint nodules that have natural But bizarre forms, chipping off the cortex (the dusky chalky coating) can make an instant sculpture

"Mock on, mock on; 'tis all in vain
You throw the sand against the wind
And the wind blows it back again"
William Blake

Fertility symbol from Oak Tree farm, Rodmersham (retrieved in 1960).

Nodule from Highsted Chalk Pit.

Left: "Bird's Head", with knapped, smoothed back. from the ditch fill, 1998 dig.

Skull of a sheep

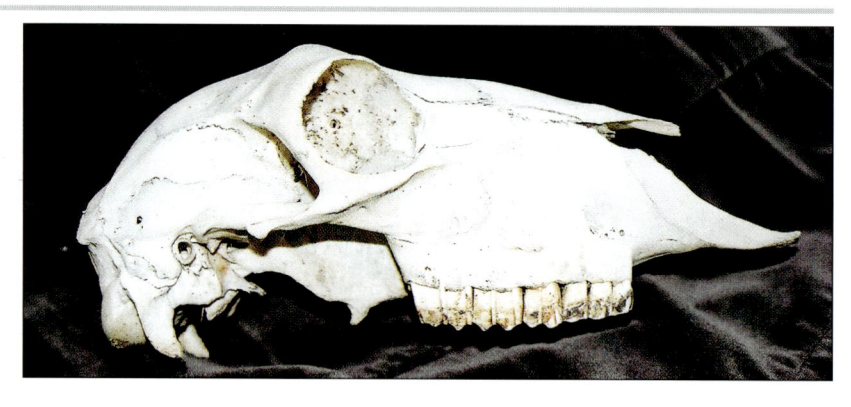

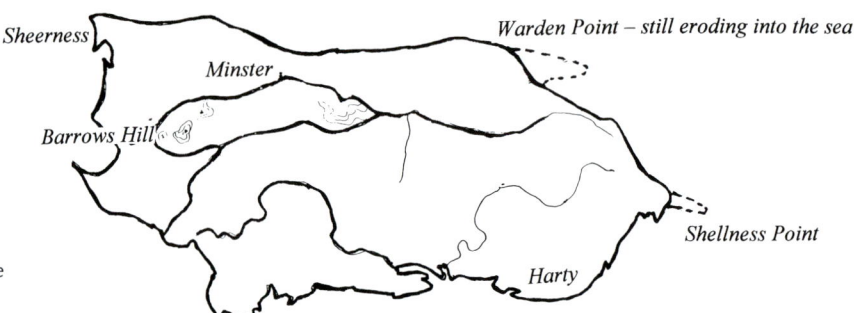

Isle of Sheppey to the same scale:-

teeth! Since I was quite young I have always thought that it looked like the skull of a sheep! With erosion from Minster cliffs and Shellness some of the outline has probably been lost. Is this a valid 'imagination', did Celtic people see shapes in islands? How could they envisage it as a map ...maybe they had a more intense spatial awareness than us ....maybe their shamans could float their conciousness out of their bodies and 'see' from above. Please do not make the mistake of closing your minds to those possibilities ....there is more to knowledge than many suppose, and many different peoples would probably tell you this is a truth. Sheppey's name does seem to come from the word 'sheep', so is it just because sheep were kept there, or does it refer to the shape?

Looking at another more important island of Kent, that of Thanet, I was struck on how much it resembled a lion.

"A lion?" Everyone will shout! It has always been suggested it was a Ram ...hence Ramsgate. But I was looking at the road map, not long after I had deduced that the streets of Kent could be ancient. Not only did my rather imaginative mind see it as a lion, it also resembled the classic representation of Leo. I immediately found a chart of the constellation of Leo and magnified it on the photocopier to match the map.

The result I found astounding. Other people since then have tried to put me down, (not an unusual occurrence it seems!) *"Oh, how could ancient people have been able to see the plan, that's total nonsense!"*

But is it? One friend who knew Thanet's archaeology better than I said rather quietly and in total surprise *"It marks Ebbsfleet with a star!"*

I had no idea at that time that Ebbsfleet was an important Neolithic/Bronze Age settlement area. Reculver is also marked by a star ...and that is proving to be ancient the Roman is set atop Iron Age ....and older, so much has been lost by erosion into the sea.

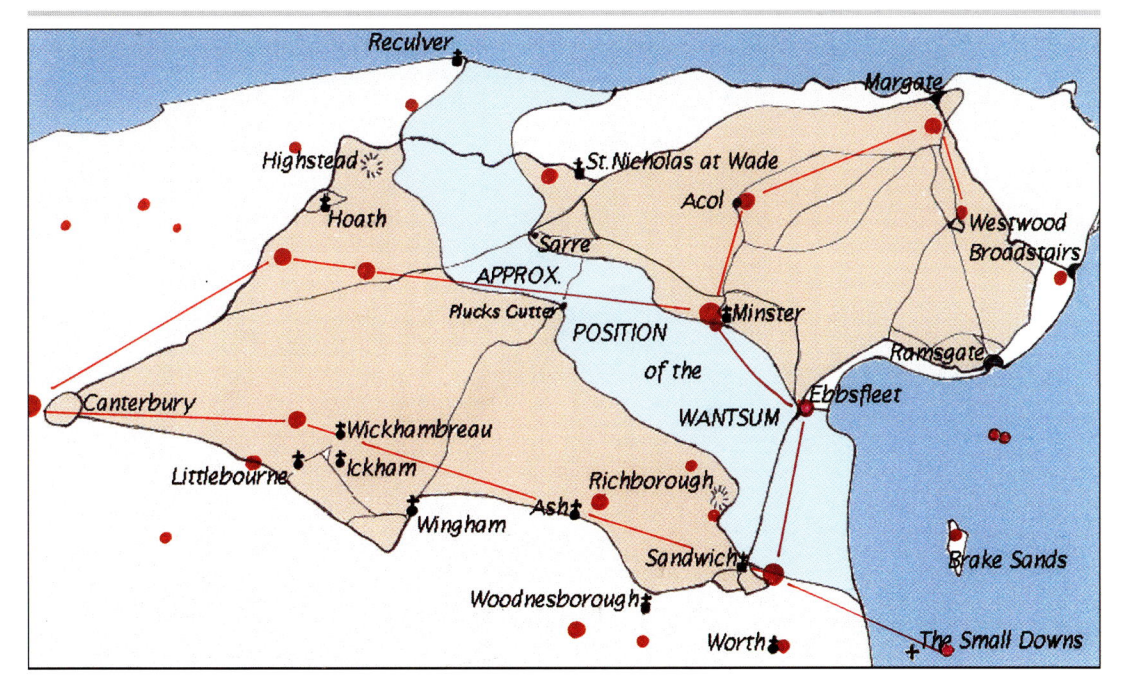

Thanet/Canterbury roads with the constellation of Leo overlaid in red
Note: none of the stars fall in the Wantsum, pure coincidence, but interesting thought that the mane of the Lion is the main, the sea!

But the resistance I was given by certain archaeologists who only seem to think with blinkers on …was considerable. My answer is keep an open mind, the Nazca Indians drew remarkable figures in the landscape interweaving their straight lines, <u>it is fact and they are there to see.</u> Just how they made them so accurately when they can only be appreciated from air space above ….is a mystery.

The mystery of Kent's possible huge figures continues, my train of thought may not be clear at first call, but hopefully by the end of the chapter it will.

Robert Burns was a Freemason and like Rudyard Kipling (another Freemason) he left clues in his poetry as to Masonic beliefs of his day. What Masons presently believe I am not wishing to know (as they seem to want to keep it secret) but what the older generation believed is more than hinted at in their poetry. They certainly knew that contact with spirits was possible and I suspect wrote down what they said:

"Oft, honoure'd with supreme command,
presided o'er the sons of light;
And by that hieroglyphic bright,
Which none but **Craftsmen** *ever saw!"*
By Robert Burns, "The farewell to the Bretheren of St. James' Lodge."

Being a scientist many people have said to me over the years *"Oh well, science precludes God"*. I will maintain that it does not at all and the more one knows in science the wider and more manifest and awe inspiring are the things we do not know.

It has been said to me many many times that in archaeology one has to deal with the *'facts'*. What are they defined as, I ask, when one is dealing with such a broad 'arch' ology that should encompass everything, science, art, theology and Man's knowledge **and imagination.** (Note, I am a Zoologist and to me Man is the specific name for the species of mankind so I do not use the idiomatic "woman" and I am not being sexist).

Lets look at some science facts of creation, now generally accepted as the truth.

Everything in the solar system and this world we live in came from our sun, (bar a few scraps of inter stellar material that may have come from outer space). In the billions of years since the sun was formed, matter has been created from elements and energy within the sun. Somehow in the beginning (and this is the mystery scientists cannot yet find the answer to) light that has **no** matter coalesced into hydrogen that **does** have a mass. From hydrogen was made helium then lithium and so on all the way down the Periodic table of elements.

When one gets as far as iron there is a problem ......to create iron the energy required would be so immense and the heat so intense that the sun would have to have been a super-nova (exploding star). Strange that in the microcosm of Man's development of civilisation, the smelting of Iron was also a turning point. Again it was the question of getting enough heat!

But I have gone forward in time too quickly ....lets think back to all the millions of years our species took to develop. Somewhere along the line our ancestors developed a highly efficient brain and somehow with the electricity of our nervous systems (through a chemical differential and electric charge) we developed a consciousness.

But the arrogance of it! Now we turn around and say *"Oh, but nothing else has a consciousness"*. How can we say that? How do we not know that all energy has a _consciousness_ ....its just that it does not have a brain and nervous system and body to express it! *"Oh, but our consciousness is from God"* I now hear the millions of religious people pipe up! That may well be, but this is where as a scientist I tend to stick within the laws of science ...as I think they are also the laws of God ...and we do not as yet fully understand them. For within those laws are some very strange things happening.

Medical research has now carried the understanding of the brain function beyond the fringe. It is on the brink of proving that telepathy is fact and that we do have a consciousness outside of our bodies. That implies that it is fact that we do have a soul. Of course you believed that any way didn't you ....? But I am trying to put it in scientific context. Somehow our mind energy (separate from our brain) has a recognition of events when the body is dead. If you do not believe that then you are disbelieving hundreds of very sane people who have courageously described things that they have experienced in near death events and they all tally in their descriptions, even in such old books like the 'Tibetan Book of the Dead'.

Now here is what all this is leading up to:

In the early 1900's a certain Frederick Bond wrote down and drew out the plan of Glastonbury Abbey. He accurately drew in all the pillars, although at that time the ruins were mostly hidden under the ground. He then went and excavated and found everything as he had drawn it. Quite scientific one might say. But then he made the mistake of admitting how he did it. I had thought at first that he had dowsed.

My *"Beyond the fringe"* chapter hopefully has allowed you all to accept that that would give a fairly accurate result .

But it was not so, Frederick Bond sat down and wrote down everything that he was told by a past monk who once lived in the Monastery. For admitting that was what he did, he was hounded out of the country and died in the U.S.A. It was, apparently, not so much the archaeologists of the day who castigated him ......but the church.

So lets consider this strange phenomenon. He accurately predicted the position of the ruins. Prediction is part of the National Curriculum for modern science ....so he got that bit with 100% of the marks! But what accepted theory did he use ...Einsteins? No, I am not joking, how do we know that time is not a moving scale and certain events 'play back'? Scientists now accept that time is a very peculiar 4th dimension that is difficult to understand. Full stop.

Another possibility:-

It has been medically proven that incoming energies can trigger the mind into certain thought patterns. Does the energy of some past soul imprint on the surroundings ....rather like on the cricket table at Harrietsham (where the magnetism had increased) ....does the game, energy of it, events, ever replay? Despite what sceptics might say, similar occurrences to Bond's experience have happened so, so, many times that we cannot pretend they do not happen. Even though they might sound "illogical" we cannot **dismiss** them when they have been recorded and observed/experienced so accurately, **that** would be an illogical thing to do.

Perhaps it was the place on Earth that Frederick Bond found himself that affected and enhanced his perceptions? Many modern-people will swear that Glastonbury does have an atmosphere. Perhaps its peaceful energy comes from the Somerset levels, the underground water energy I have mentioned before. Many people will profess that they have felt a surge of energy in the crypt of Canterbury Cathedral and I will not dispute that either. It is standing so close to the Stour.

Another point to consider, is it educationally correct that 'Classic Archaeologists' should ignore 'New Age' people?.....for how do they know they have not got a fair bit of the truth? All human experience (not just arte-facts) is archaeology. I think the recent programme about a sea-henge off the Norfolk coast brought that home to people. Most people I spoke to thought the henge should never have been removed and were disturbed by the high-handedness of those who thought it should be 'saved'. In other words they sided with the protesters. Now it has actually been put back into the sea! In the recent excavations along the Channel Tunnel Rail Link through Kent, there was a considerable amount of archaeology found at Blue Bell Hill. It was already known that this was an ancient sacred site near the White Horse Stone and it was not really surprising that a Neolithic longhouse was found there. What was somewhat disturbing was how hush-hush it was kept, C.T.R.L. were not at first willing to have many visitors. It was also not made public knowledge that around 30 sarsen stones were found on that site. *"All natural"* as the Senior Archaeologist termed them. But, although the stones are "natural" their position often is not. In this case they had probably been moved and covered during farming, but where were they originally? Part of the long lost sarsen avenue? Had the presence of these stones been made public perhaps (as I think CTRL may have worried about) protesters might have slowed the engineering up. But, it is our country, our heritage, should not everything that is being done be open? A delicate balance of different views no doubt, but it needs deeper thought, and in my opinion not enough serious thought is being given to some views .....for they *could* be close to the truth!

Imaginary reconstruction of the Neolithic longhouse, excavated on Blue Bell Hill is the first one ever to be found in Kent! Such a pity no TV footage was taken and so few people allowed to see it in situ, even though all that remained were dark stains in the soil.

That site around the White Horse Stone has considerable energy fields so I am told. Sometimes it just buzzes with a static ....is that why there is a well recorded 'ghost' on the main road through it?

So many of my references have been about the power of static electricity in water. Woodstock, Kent, has underground water and I am sure something from the combined affect of that water and the great age of occupation of the site does affect sensitive people. I will hasten to add it has always been a positive affect.

Now I will admit my "Bond" experience :- when we were first investigating the site I had a very vivid and technicoloured dream three nights running. It was

Laying out Highsted ......dream of the past.

exactly the same each night as if an energy field were somehow triggering thought patterns in my brain. I rarely, if ever, have repeat dreams.

In my dream, there were small people (around five feet in stature), in biscuit coloured tunics and black fringed hair cuts, busy laying out Highsted. They had extraordinarily long poles (slightly flexible) and they thought to me (I did not hear them speak). *"You must get the diagonals correct."* I felt an extraordinary feeling of friendship and happiness coming from them as I watched them measuring up the land, not only just there but further across the valley also.

It was from mulling on this very vivid repeat dream that I got the idea of lines and diagonals in the landscape. I **had not**, before then, read anything much at all about 'ley lines'. The realisation came to me almost like a bolt from the blue, a distant memory, and the Zoological theory that we might have some 'ancestral memories' gelled as a distinct reality. If monarch butterfly second generation descendants can remember the way back to Mexico from Canada on a flight path their grand-parents made the season before, why should our far superior complex brains not remember a few ancestral facts and customs?

Diagonals, why were they important? ....if one gets the diagonal and the side measurements correct the corner (of a square) becomes a good right angle. Did these ancients know the disciplines of geometry and Pythagoras? Where were the squares? Certainly there was one at the northern end of the Woodstock site. But looking at the map I visualised a much bigger one and the diagonals were almost exact, still in place as footpaths and a landmark church stood in the centre, Kingsdown. But that present church is very modern, St. Catherine's, completed in 1877, it stands on a medieval site perhaps on an even older one? But why did my mind think there was a significance in that square? Well might you ask.

For sometime I had suspected that there were ancient settlement sites around Newnham (mentioned by George Payne), Lynsted and at Timbold Hill. Together with Highsted they formed a square. Why was this square significant? ….It still flummoxed me, I had no idea ….and for nearly 10 years pondered on the problem ….the little people did not appear again to help me!!! But I had to laugh at the Freemasons poems …… *"the circle the line and the square!"* Although I had still to find a circle. But it was not till I had to teach astronomy at school that I suddenly realised where there was a square in the natural world, or rather an apparent square ……. *The Great Square of Pegasus!*

"Now she has really gone beyond the pale" ….does someone shout? But why should it not be possible that ancient Celts, a nation of sea-farers, steering by the stars, that they might have laid out the land on star plans? Sophisticated, spatially aware, dyslexics, not able to write things down in the usual way but able to draw on the landscape with an amazing precision? The centre of Celtic learning and philosophy, where the Continental Celts came to learn the art ….of astronomy?

To tell the whole story of the pale horse ….needs another chapter!

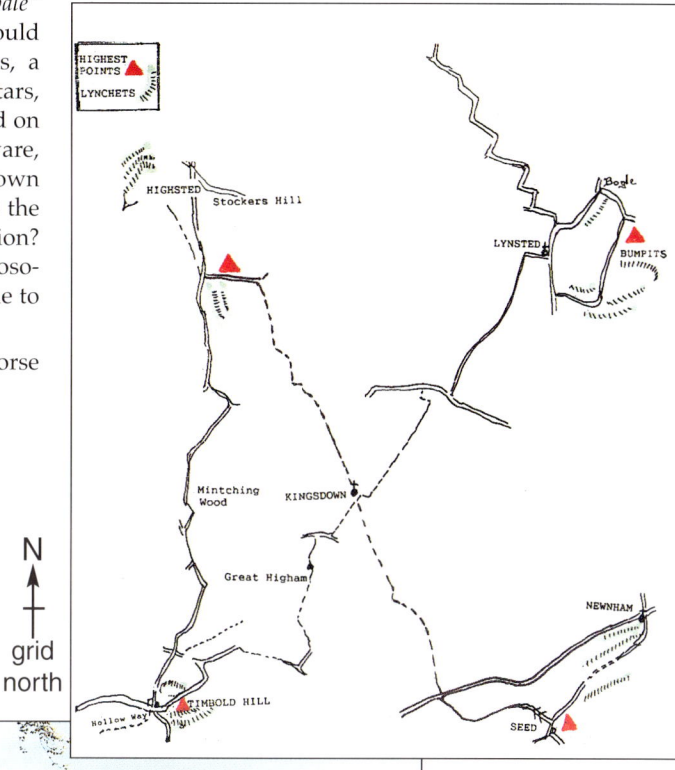

The Bumpits, near Lynsted, in 1986.

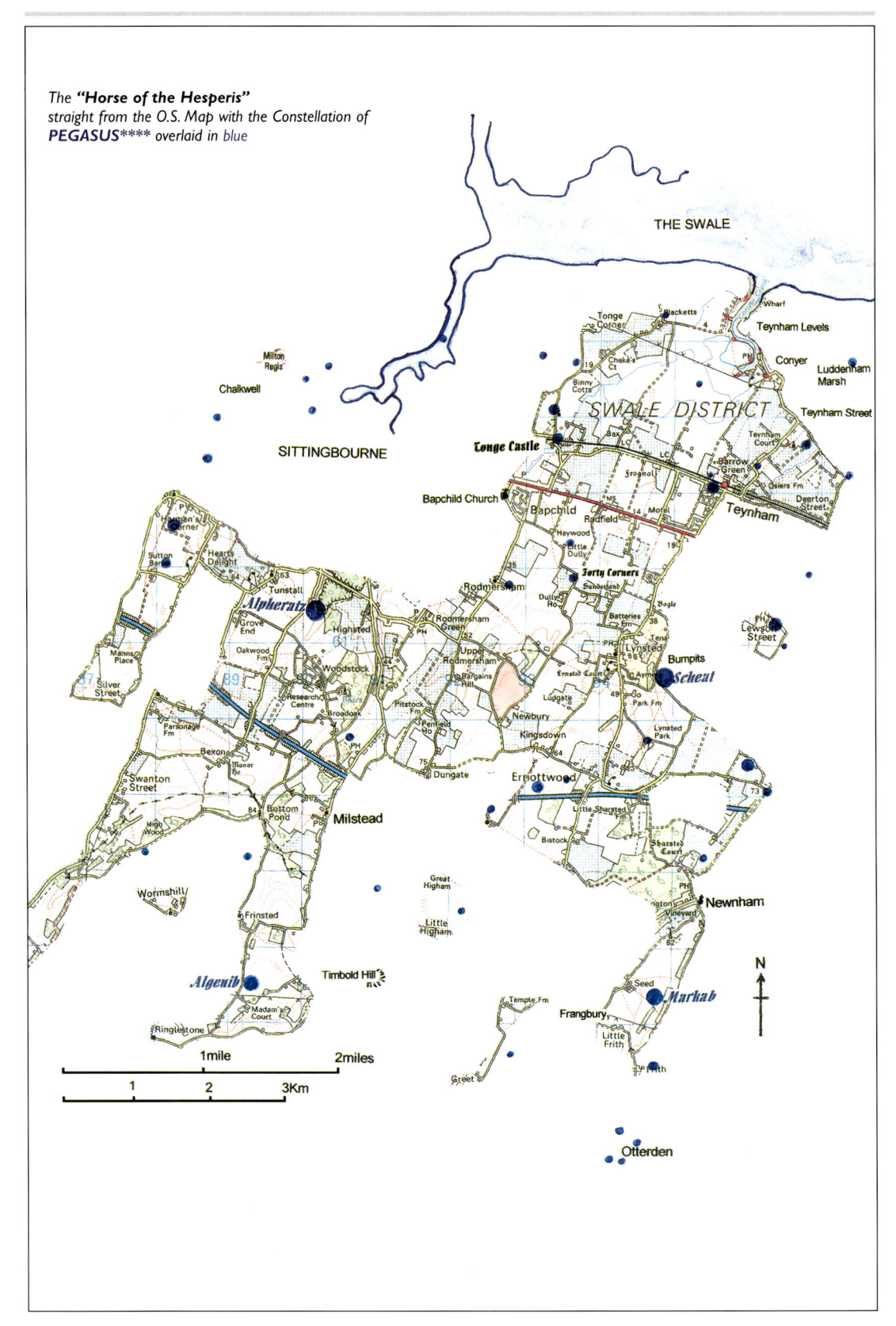

The **"Horse of the Hesperis"**
straight from the O.S. Map with the Constellation of
PEGASUS**** overlaid in blue

Chapter 13

The Horse of the Hesperis

Having realised that the square of these ancient sites was possibly based on the Great Square of Pegasus, I immediately searched for an accurate star plan of the constellation and enlarged it to fit the O.S. Map. I was momentarily disappointed. It did not fit! But then I realised that it did if the star *Algenib* corresponded to Frinsted and not Timbold Hill!

Frinsted was another possible site, very close to Timbold Hill, that also had an interesting banking system and position ….but would they be so close together? Knowing that Caesar had written that Celtic buildings were *"everywhere"* the answer seemed to be yes, it was possible. The area of Frinsted and Timbold Hill commands views across most of East Kent from Grain and Essex across to Herne Bay and the Canterbury downs. They stand close to the Wychling trackway, on Rawlings Street (that connects to Teynham) and the street through the Doddington valley that leads north-eastwards to Faversham and south-westwards to Hollingbourne.

Four years after I had realised the possible importance of Frinsted (and reported into the County Archaeology Department of my observations) four gold quarter staters were found, and later (in 2000A.D.) two other Celtic coins nearer to Timbold Hill!

The metal detectorist, Peter Barker, did not know of my predicted sites when he originally found the first four coins and I was later able to introduce him to the adjacent land-owner who wanted a reliable detectorist to investigate his land.

The other two Celtic coins which were found were also *extremely* interesting. A silver Tincommius with TINC inscribed on the face and a bull on the obverse is only the second Tincommius to ever surface in Kent! He was an Atrebate ruler from Sussex!

The second unit was issued by the joint rulers Eppilus and Verica, also Atrebates! One side shows a head facing right with VIR CO inscribed, the other

> *"Time present and time past*
> *Are both perhaps present in time future*
> *And time future contained in time past,*
> *If all time is eternally present*
> *All time is unredeemable."*
> T.S.Eliot

Here is Peter's excellent photograph and his description of the coins:-

"The smallest quarter stater featured is of the Kent ruler Vosenios of the Cantii tribe. Little is known of him except that he issued coins in a characteristiclly Kentish style similar to those of Dubnovellaunus. Vosenios ruled Kent during the late 1st Century B.C. and early 1st Century A.D. The 3 larger coins are Gallo-Belgic type E staters, which were imported from the Continent and were some of the earliest coins to circulate in Britain. They were made in Gaul and imported into S.E.England from @150 B.C. onwards.

side shows Capricorn facing left with EPPI-COMF inscribed around. Both these two coins date from a similar age as the gold staters, between 10B.C. - 20A.D.

The other places to look for sites according to my astronomy co-ordinates would be Seed, near Newnham, which seems to be the star point equivalent to *Markab*. Bumpits, near Lynsted, equivalent to *Scheat* and of course Woodstock which equals *Alpheratz*. No coins have come up on the Woodstock site at all despite our extensive trawling. Bumpits has a possible meaning of *"bone pits"* which might suggest it was a burial place. I only hope that if metal detectorists have already found items that they now declare them as Peter has, for that is the correct way to do things.

But how do I know that the star pattern was even fixed round that way? I admit I do not …..but the configuration rotates remarkably well and strangely, the research on the meaning of Seed lists the name stems *Schede, Shethe, scead*. How uncannily similar to *Scheat*! The name of one of the main stars of the Pegasus square.

The meaning of scaed = boundary. Again that is very curious, do the markers indicate an important area and the whole of the enclosed area was where the people lived ….within the limits of their star sign? Since the time several years ago, when I had the vivid dream of *the surveyors*, I have not had many inspired thoughts ….

But whilst I was writing this book I was pondering on what to call this chapter …. Epona? Invicta? The White Horse? I suddenly wrote down what just sprang into my mind, I found I was writing without registering what the words were and I then had to go back and read them ….

"We wanted you to know that the Horse of the Hesperis is our home. We made the outline and dug the shoreline to make it fit better. The horse does not need its legs although they are there, its importance lies in its head. It loves like no other animal and it remembers our souls. It has no reason to distrust Man if treated correctly and it is the centre of our tradition and life."

If the above came out of my subconscious mind …..it still makes sense; the words key in to several possibilities. Perhaps if time is like a sliding corridor perhaps something from the past *had* communicated the truth to me. Look at the outline and road system/footpaths with the overlying Pegasus constellation. The head is the most convincing area ….but I have 'cheated' a little! The constellation of Lacerta I have moved down closer to the square of Pegasus….but it is as if *that* is where it should be on the ground plan. The zigzag road, Forty Corners (as it is known locally) is very curious, it almost suggests a 'cut-here' instruction. Many horses heads *have* been found buried separately on Iron Age sites (e.g. recently one was found in the Chatham Dockyard dig). The pattern of that road goes round field boundaries and field boundaries, square and of that size are often *Iron Age!* There are other circumstantial facts that suggest it is an Iron Age plan.

David Perkins (Thanet Trust) has remarked that evidence he has found suggests the Thanet Celts seem to be linked to the Parisii tribe (Belgic Celts from around Paris). Parisii Celts were also found in Yorkshire and were responsible for the chariot burials, (if you missed reading my Preface go back and check). The Highsted quarry had what appears to have been a chariot burial ….one of the only ones found outside Yorkshire?

When this name *"Hesperis"* appeared in front of me I did not know what it meant. Vaguely I could remember a poem ….but that was the *"Wreck of the Hesperus"* a poem by Longfellow. I looked the word up in *"Encyclopaedia Britanica"*. The Greek word is *Hesperos* meaning of the west and particularly the morning (or evening star) which is of course Venus. Hesperis is the <u>female</u> noun! How uncanny, I thought to myself, I did not know any of that, but **I was aware** that the sacred horse of the Iron Age Celts was Epona, **and it was always female!**

"The legs of the Horse are not important…" that seemed to refer to the ground plan and look at the abstract design of the legs on the coins! In one book, *"Collins pocket Guide to Stars & Planets"*, Pegasus is drawn differently:

Remarkably similar to the configuration on the coins?

Round the other way ….but that means little when one realises that the die for the coin was round the other way. Things get reversed and I am almost certain that visual images get stored in a reversed form in our brains and we are oftern unaware that is so.

So had I been given the truth? It seemed to ring so uncannily true. People who were brilliant historical novelists, such as Sir Walter Scott, reputedly, somehow, tapped the past (Frederick Bond fashion) to obtain an authentic ring to their stories .

Either I had been given information from a source outside of myself **or** my subconscious had tapped knowledge, perhaps an ancestral knowledge, within my brain that my conscious thinking process was unaware of.

Using my own thoughts (at least I think they are mine) to unlock the mystery still further, I think it is highly likely that Iron Age Celts really *did* look upon the place in which they lived, the whole landscape itself, and hold it as *sacred*. Thinking back to similarities in Celtic gods and Hindu pantheism, I think it is possible that there was no central 'temple', the whole landscape would be the temple and worship could have been at small home shrines much as it is in Hindu society today. Places like Stonehenge were likely astronomical observatories rather than 'temples.' Underlying the Iron Age is of course millennia of older Celtic tradition where underground passage tombs and fogous were important. But perhaps in the Iron Age that older darker 'mystery' had lessened in importance? For one other uncanny meaning of *Hesperis* listed in the encyclopaedia was that it meant "The Bringer of Light!" and yet another meaning was "The Guardian of the Golden Apples".

So did the astronomical (and astrological) knowledge of the Iron Age British Celts put them in a very important position with the rest of the world? Both astronomy and astrology were classed as a similar (if not the same) skill in those days, so did aspiring priests of the day travel to Britain to study the science and learn the secrets (the Golden Apples)?

In the Roman written accounts we are told that this did happen and that Britain was a centre of Celtic religious knowledge. So likewise, the legendary account of Jesus travelling to Britain in his youth may be correct.

"There are other sheep not of this fold" I always like to think He meant the Celts!

Getting back to the plan of 'The Horse'. The heart shaped road system, in the right place for its heart, has always intrigued me. I was not unduly surprised, therefore, when researching aerial photographs at the Royal Commission HQ in Swindon, that shadowy 'buildings' were in evidence in that area of Upper Rodmersham.

Brian Philp dug part of a Roman Villa in that 'heart' area near Little Newbury in 1985. Dr. Paul Wilkinson has done geophysical surveys that show that particular villa is quite extensive. A farmer friend tells us the plough always snags on something near Scuttington and shadows of possible buildings show near Bargains Hill. Pitstock Farm has a definite crop mark, in fact two or more.

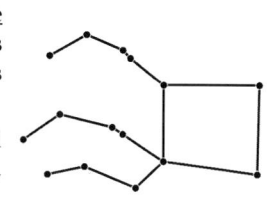

Now that the 'square' has had most of its orchards grubbed out – people should be keeping a watchful eye for crop marks and be scanning every aerial photograph as sometimes may show on just a few days in the year. I am certain the density of sites in that area will be high.

The 'head' area has already produced a few finds and Dr. Wilkinson has already located a major site near the 'nose'. Remember, sites are often one on top of another.

Romans built on Celtic sites and quite often manor houses seem to be built on Roman sites.

Barrow Green speaks for itself, but possibly some ploughed out barrows have not yet been located. Teynham Street, I am sure, will prove one day to have been an important port (if anyone cares to investigate).

Lynsted, "the horse brass" on the horse's chest, has numerous lynchets or banks and Bumpits certainly looks interesting (see picture in previous chapter).

Lewson Street (under a star) is another small square of lanes and it's possible name meaning sounds intriguing "Lady's (or Mistress's) mound". (The dictionary definition means a 'freemason's son' which I find rather amusing!) But there is no mound there now it is dead flat!

Legends surrounding horses abound. I mentioned afore that the Hindu legends and Celtic ones could be similar. The Hindus say that in his last avatar (or incarnation) the Lord Vishnu comes riding on his white horse, Kalki, brandishing his sword like a comet! Vishnu is traditionally God of Creation, but comes at the end, as if in his awful role reversal, equivalent to Shiva = destruction. Is it not possible that Hengist 'cashed-in' on this Celtic fear of the Great Destroyer and used the emblem of the white horse =Invicta? It would explain how he swept the country with little opposition as he came in around the time of a reappearance of Halley's comet. Perhaps the Celts truly believed he was a god and in their abject fear, reverted to their old religion of sacrifice to appease his wrath. In the book *"Roman Bath Discovered"* Barry Cunliffe describes how a head of a girl was found in a bread oven of the sacked Roman city as though the desperate Celts had made a last ditch sacrificial appeal to their gods.

Banks near the star point of Frinsted and close to where the gold staters surfaced.

Like Hitler in the last war, who borrowed a good and lucky emblem, the Hindu swastika, and reversed its meaning to an evil symbol, Hengist used the Invicta as a symbol of his savage victory. But the Celtic Horse of the Hesperis was around the other way, instead of facing west to the setting sun and destruction, it faced east to the rising sun …and hope? It is the same way around as the Uffington Horse.

You may not believe that this Horse of the Hesperis really exists, just as you may have dismissed the Leo of Thanet and the sheep of Sheppey ….but there are a lot of people out there who may see as I do, that it is a distinct possibility! And the more sites that are found on target as I have suggested ….the more likely it will become.

At present, at the turn of the Millenium, archaeologists of Kent and Sussex are arguing about where the Roman Invasion actually took place ….it would be as well for them to stop arguing and do more investigative archaeology to establish more facts on the Kentish Celts! There is so much that we do not know.

Is it not likely that all these sites, especially where these coins have surfaced, are very important? And no one has looked in detail!

Perhaps readers have noticed all the 'steds' mentioned do not have an 'A'. That may have significance in that they are not Saxon but from sted meaning place, or an O.E. word steda = steed, back to horses again!

Yet another name for horse is caple or capul (cabel=hill?), and is close to the words cape (a point of land running into the sea) and the Latin caballus =horse and caput =head. Perhaps the hills were seen as horses and also as places of worship giving us yet another word chapel. In Malta (an important Neolithic centre) Gebel is a stony hill and they often have little chapels. So horses, heads, hills, and places of worship are all mixed up together!

Mystery solved to some extent? …but it always goes ahead of us ….like a rainbow.

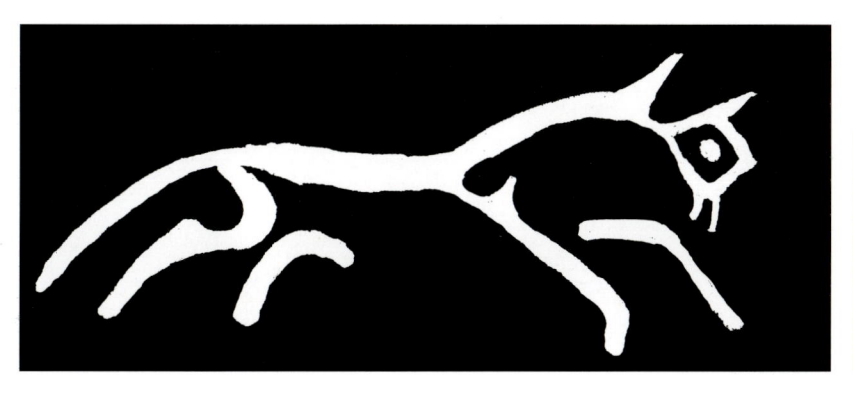

When our Past benigns our Future
And our Present stays with us
In a sea of understanding
Love, Hope and Trust
Then Time stands still
Like the Horse on the hill
L.F.2001-06-25

STONES of EASTLING and SEED

- **Stones as shown on the 1909 map**
  Firstly, do these 'stones' on the map represent Sarsens?
  Do any of them still exist in their 'rightful position'? I have been unable to find any!
  The positions shown **do not** seem to be random and as large sarsens were important to Bronze and Neolithic Age people it is **logical** to assume they were set in significant places.
  It is sad that the major disruption of their positions (complete disappearance!) has only happened in the last Century.

Large sarsen under North side of Newnham Church.

Large sarsen by the roadside at Warren Street, Lenham, Kent.

Chapter 14

Circles of the Mind

Although the Medway Valley is a classified Megalithic area there are no recorded circles. On most maps of such sites in England even a circle as at Coldrum Barrow seems to get left out! The Victorians and past people of Kent did a grand job in removing most of the smaller stones! There may well have been stone circles on Blue Bell Hill at Westfield Sole and in other places. All that we have got left now are remnants of what was. Now even archaeologists say *"Oh, they are just stones that have been moved by the farmers!"*

"The windmill sails are turning like a wheel within a wheel......"

If one realises that the naturally occurring Kentish sarsens, which are a very hard sandstone found largely above the chalk layers, in what are termed geologically the Hucking beds, have been moved around by Man for at least 5000 years; it is not surprising that they do not appear to be in specific easily recognisable patterns.

First moved and arranged by Neolithic and Bronze Age people …left largely in place by the Iron Age and Roman, avidly destroyed or sat on by churches in the middle Ages, blown up by the Royal Engineers in the 19th and 20th centuries, moved by farmers, disregarded as 'natural' in the late 20th century by archaeologists and sold for garden centres to this day! Is it surprising that we have no man made stone circles left in Kent?

Lower Medway Archaeological Group have surveyed a scatter of stones on the horn like hill of Westfield Wood, just to the east of Blue Bell Hill and immediately above the Upper White Horse stone. The lower White Horse stone was blown up in the 1800's. There are well over 20 lying in Westfield. From our survey it does not look as if they were in a circle unless several have been moved (which is highly likely!)

In Impton Wood, Walderslade, just half a mile distant, there are a lot more! Some of these are as large as the Lower Kit's Coty stones and with two piles of 20 or so in each they represent a sorry, neglected tumble of our Neolithic heritage all daubed with yellow painted graffiti! *"Oh, they have been dragged off the fields, they are not significant local archaeologists tell me!"* Fields? Where are the fields? Frith Wood just to the south is ancient woodland they are spending no end of money 'moving' it to allow the motorway extension through! How about recording and caring for the stones of Impton Wood?

Some of the Impton Stones in Impton/Tunbury Wood

The second pile

Is there any record of where these were located last century? Is it a disrupted chambered tomb? What is the semi-circular bank adjacent at Tunbury?

Is there any record of the size, position and the number that the Royal Engineers destroyed in Nashenden Woods last century? These are all questions that warrant investigation and recording by anyone interested enough to do it.

I just hope it stuns people and brings home how much of Kent's ancient archaeology has been neglected. Few seem to have been interested in the pre-history, only in Romans! Many people living in Walderslade literally have Neolithic and Bronze Age archaeology in their back-gardens!

But fortunately these sarsens were not totally neglected, some one was interested enough to mark 'stones' on the 1909 maps. Now that my knees are failing me and I find walking so difficult, walking along all the footpaths and locating them all, seeing if any are still there and what they tell us ....is for other interested folk to do.

I am just going to point out to you that they are marked on the maps, and hopefully enthuse you, to get out and about and have a look! Be sure to take a note book and pencil and perhaps a camera ....and be sure to ask permission if any are not on footpaths!

Take a look at the section of map from the Eastling/Doddington area. Look at the circle near Dunstall House. Are you going to say that that circle is 'natural'? The position of the house looks as if it should have a stone under it.

Now I have suggested in the previous chapter that there could have been star plans laid out in Kent .... does this one look like a constellation?

Perhaps the constellation of *Capricorn?*

Or does the 'tear drop' arrangement near Dunstall = *Corona Borealis?*

So many stars as we now see them have moved relative to the others, so many stones on Eastling may have been moved. There are so many variables to juggle with ....I am leaving it to your brilliant brain-boxes (with the aid of computers) to solve .... The Circles of the Mind!!!

I mentioned before the possible link between the images on the coins and what the Celts saw around them.

So how about the Capricorn on the obverse of the silver Eppilus & Verica coin? Is there indeed a representation of *Capricorn* somewhere in the vicinity? The local name of Mintching Wood, that in the 1700's stretched from Timbold Hill to Golden Wood and nearly down to Watling Street, gives the amusing suggestion that somewhere it housed a coin mint! From the coins that have now been found the question arises whether it was a Celtic one of Vosenios? The mint of Dumnovellaunus has never been found either.

One thing is certain, the Celts were definitely into astronomy/astrology and were aware of the stars and considered them important enough to put on their coins.

One additional fact about stone circles (that also helped me to think up the title of this chapter) is described in a book called *"The Circles of Silence"* by Don Robbins, published in 1985 by Souvenir Press. Don Robbins took his scientific instruments inside many of the well known stone circles and instead of there being a background chatter of radiation …there was nothing….. a flat line of silence! Scientifically this silence is abnormal.

So it would appear that whoever set them up knew that this was a fact. Perhaps a stone circle that somehow negates Earth energy interference allows the mind to tune into and be more open to different energies?

Another place that intrigues me, and perhaps needs keen time tracker archaeologists to research, is Stalisfield Green just S.E. of Eastling. It is pronounced *'Stars field'* and again is high plateau with a commanding view ….so did it have any stones?

Getting back to Eastling, its name derivation is strangely not *east* but more likely *Esla* meaning *'of God'*. So did the *'people of God'* live there? Or was it the ling = *line* of God, as I explained before? I scarcely wish to hazard a guess as to which direction the Eastling line went …. I will leave that for you to have fun working out! Perhaps it was the N➔S line from Doddington church through St. Martins, Frith (now disappeared without trace).

Incidentally, there are various local 'co-incidences' that I find somewhat amusing. Several of the churches are dedicated to John the Baptist and Rodmersham Church was built by the Knights of St. John of Malta (John the Baptist is their saint). He was noted for saying *"make the paths straight"*…so did his name get attached to churches that were on important *ancient lings,* did they get dedicated to the 'ley' saint to Christianise the 'evil' as medieval people thought the electro-magnetic energy was? If so it is not surprising that Doddington Church (Doddington could be linked to Dodeman, the layer of the leys) gets the more unusual dedication that of *"The Beheading of John the Baptist"*. It is a church that is reputed to have several ley lines.

Circles of the mind ….. this is a short chapter ……I leave it to others to extend it and find out more, for there is so much that has never been discovered! There is enough here for thoughts to start circling in your minds.

Is what I have said all nonsense ….or **is** there some truth in it?

Whatever, there are three roughly circular sites that I think warrant further investigation and all three are important in establishing some truth behind the theory of ley lines and might show the sceptics that so called 'medieval' sites may well be much older .

1. Tonge Castle: already featured in Chapter 4. Its moat was sectioned circa 1965 but they did not cut across the northern side. Now, with modern technology and methods the exact age of the moat might be established. The FACT that there are at least four sarsen stones in the vicinity might suggest that the site is indeed Neolithic ….yet the sarsens were not even mentioned in the report! It is on a line from Tonge to Frinsted and through to the Ringlestone. It is also under a star on the Horses head ….if that theory of mine is nonsense then I challenge someone to prove it. (I do not mind if they do ….but it is a strange coincidence!)

*Ref. B. Davison. Medieval Archaeology Vol. XVI 1972 p.123.

Lossenden microlith x 2

Actual size

Castle Toll - looking east from the ploughed bailey to all that remains of the main mound. 1996.

2. Castle Toll: on the Kent/Sussex border, near Newenden. It was looked at in 1972* and labelled 'medieval' but very little evidence bar a few pieces of pottery were found. It was then stated that it was unlikely to be a 'hillfort' (a statement I entirely agree with as it is on the Rother levels) but it is the ideal position for an ancient 'cranog'. The real pity is that the county has allowed the farmer to plough the 'bailey' of the mound and it is slowly getting reduced. Surely it could be maintained so much better as just grazing particularly now when some farmers are paid not to farm, but to 'set aside'? Would it not be infinitely more sensible to pay for 'set asides' on known archaeological sites? One interesting observation is that Castle Toll is on a due north alignment from Fairlight Church. We were told by one of the grave diggers that there was a large 'blue' sarsen (probably Wadhurst blue stone) in one part of the graveyard and he could not dig graves in that area. Just a mile north of the church near Guestling there is a manmade tump (it could be an iron working but it is remarkably symmetrical). Due north of that is a hill called Ludley and due north of that is Great Knelle, a hill that stands looking over the levels. I showed this S→N line to a Sussex archaeologist and his observant eye picked out the next point, which is of course Castle Toll. "What's that?" he queried." *A supposed Medieval Castle*" I replied. *"Strange, its in the wrong place for a medieval castle ......"* he mused …so perhaps he is right and it is not medieval. Certainly people have travelled that way for a very long time for I picked up a few worked flints, here is a microlith that is most likely Mesolithic some 8000 years B.C.

3. Binbury: standing at the top of the Queens Down near Detling. (See Chapter 11 page 81).

This is my third interesting castle that needs further investigation and excavation to establish its origins. Again I would guess that it is ancient (Neolithic? Bronze Age?)

Only thorough investigation would tell. Is it the 'dot' or mound that gives the name to Detling, and is the 'ling' meaning a line?

So, when people trot out the cliché **"Oh, ley hunters line sites of different ages"**, to be perfectly accurate they need to retract those words.

Most of the churches and castle mottes <u>could</u> be ancient. Until firm and conclusive evidence is produced to establish the age of all sites then that cliché is not a valid one nor is it logical! It seems designed to be a 'wool-over-the-eyes' statement and makes me wonder if some people have a policy of ignoring the existence of a great number of very ancient sites that go back far into antiquity.

Many archaeologists need to circle their minds back to the truth and perhaps look at archaeology with fresh eyes!

Even on the recent Channel Tunnel Rail Track, where sites investigated were said to have all their archaeology done, one wonders how much was circled

Sarsen stone at the Bluebell Hill Rail Track site.

All is not lost! The Bronze Age/I.A. settlement site gave indications it extends SW under the A229 and out onto the ridge above Cossington. In the eadish perhaps it can be investigated? (See chapt. 16) Perhaps there will be another longhouse?

around. We were told that the 30 or so sarsen stones found on site close to the Neolithic Longhouse discovered at Bluebell Hill were all "natural". Had they been established as being in an ancient 'sacred' position no doubt public pressure would have been born to change the position of the Rail Track or at least hold up the construction. That may be the reason why 'circles' of words may have been spun to convince everyone that these stones were 'natural' and therefore 'unimportant'?

'Circles of the mind' in archaeology are continually turning, relentlessly. As this book goes to press the enormity of the 'Valetta Convention' just signed in 2001 by our Government, ostensibly puts paid to any 'amateur' archaeology! It is pointless doing any investigative archaeology on a freelance basis as only government 'licenced' archaeology by 'licenced' archaeologists will be able to take place! Even 'geophys' investigation, field walking, aerial photography and certainly metal detection, may be banned! So my attempts to encourage enthusiasm, interest and involvement seem completely misguided! Farmers will apparently be allowed to inadvertently plough out barrows etc., but not be allowed to field-walk and retrieve any artefacts that might alert us to what is there.

Even countries like Malta (where the 'Convention' presumably arose) can be in ignorance of what they are losing. A Maltese relative of mine has seen (to his horror!) construction workers hastily fill in and destroy Punic graves etc. because to tell the government would mean loss of the site, time and money. (Punic people are the ancient Carthaginians who buried their dead in sarcophagi, similar to the Egyptians). It seems government compensation needs to be financially adequate to prevent the destruction of heritage and be an incentive to report finds.

But what is worse, destroying statues with the world watching, as did the Taliban of Afghanistan, or letting things get destroyed on the quiet or even in total ignorance that they exist at all? We are perhaps in the latter category and we ought to know better but it seems we shall go on losing our archaeology with our heads in the proverbial sand (or should it be plough soil?)! The line *"Ancient sites are best left alone"* still echoes from chapter 5.

Having been once reproved by a top archaeologist for mentioning 'politics' in archaeology, I now ask can it be avoided? Isn't everything affected/effected by politics and money? With a heavy heart I leave you to read chapters 15 and 16, sadly much of it becomes defunct; amateurs will be banned; Europe wins; will much of our heritage get lost under a similar attitude as the 19th century master of Cobham Hall?

Above: Digging in Hastings, the garden of Rossetti House.
This is an 'aerial' view from the next door window. Michael Greenhalgh is working on the Victorian brick path found under modern concrete. After it had been drawn accurately using the metre grid the bricks were lifted and the next context excavated. Many of the items pictured on pages 110-111 came from a 17th-18th century rubbish pit beneath that area.

Lenham volunteers operating the Kent Archaeological Society resistivity meter on a very warm week-end, July 2001. No significant features were found but early indications are there could be something under the field to the right (east) but little, if anything, under the new Community Centre site that they are surveying.

Chapter 15

Hints and advice for Young (and Old) Time Trackers.

This chapter is a brief run down of the way to find/do/report on your own archaeology.

1. JOIN A GROUP: this is important if not essential and one will find like-minded people who are helpful and well informed and fun to be with. Here is the Hastings group H.A.A.R.G. on site at Glossam's Place Beckley, E.Sussex:-

The figure standing on the left is supposed to be a likeness of the East Sussex County Archaeologist, he found the site for us and was a great help in planning it. But the major work was done in combined effort from all the members.

The site is a moated medieval manor house overlaying a Romano-British iron working. As more walls are found the team is consolidating them so that eventually the site will be able to be viewed by the general public. It is on Forestry Commission land in a beautiful wooded spot.

2. ASK PERMISSION of the land owner if you are interested in a site or area. This is an essential. Footpaths only have a metre wide public access and the

> *"Dig and delve in your own backyard*
> *For buckles and bobbins, coin or shard*
> *Bottles and pipes and bones of old*
> *One Man's rubbish is another one's gold!"*
> L.F.2001-01-06

H.A.A.R.G. dig at
Glossams Place, Beckley Wood.
Summer of 1999.

interesting sherd you may notice is bound to be beyond that! Remember all finds are the initial property of the land owner.

3. RESEARCH: this is also essential. Books, newspapers, maps, estate and tithe maps, aerial photographs, bills of sale, reports etc. can variously be found in local libraries, county archives and museums. (Often your local archaeology group will have its own collection of books and local finds .)

Unless you research the area and your possible 'site' from maps/local information you may later be disappointed in finding it is not something 'old' after all! The classic let down would be to get excited and interested about an 'old' earthwork in a wood ….only to find it was a neglected section of railway embankment made redundant in the 1960's!

4. RECORDING: make sure you record all your observations and finds! Keep a note book, learn to draw (or else record things on the scanner which is very easy and efficient) and perhaps attend courses to learn how to do things.

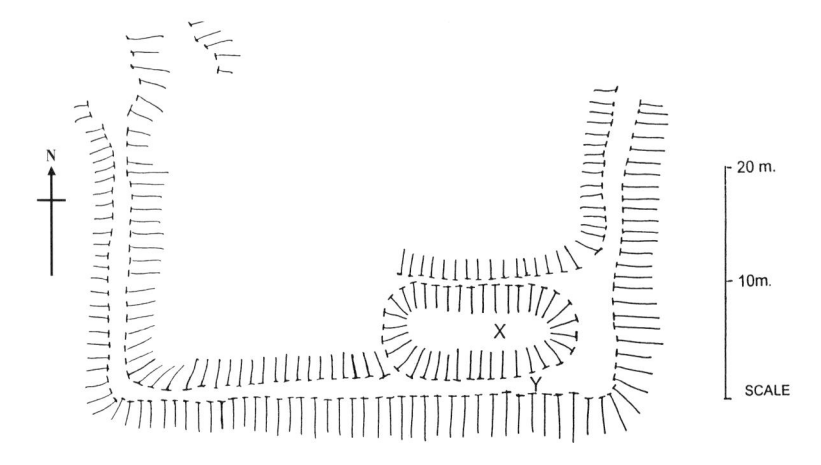

A previously unrecorded ditched enclosure near Milstead.

Approx. depth at 'X' and 'Y' = 1.30 m.

To make notes and draw diagrammatically is not difficult if you learn the basics .

5. READING/COURSES: most counties and local authorities have evening and week-end courses for you to attend. Some courses give you credits towards a degree or certificate. Learning to survey, recognise and describe artefacts, operate geophysics equipment are all useful skills and much can be found in books.

6. FIELD WALKING: perhaps one of the most useful skills and occupations for volunteer archaeologists. This I find one of the most rewarding and is a way of getting you outside in the fresh air and in touch with archaeology at 'grass roots' level. It is also a skill and occupation that is very good for the younger archaeologists as there is no dangers involved (so long as you keep away from electricity pylons and wear gloves). Always ask permission from the land owner! It is best to grid out the area using pegs or canes.

7. METAL DETECTING: this often appeals to younger archaeologists and more often males than females (cannot quite see why but that is fact!) As is standard archaeology, join a group! Make sure you have the landowner's permission (remember all the finds are his/hers in the first instance). Never trawl on a known and registered SMR site unless you get permission. Always record where you find things (using a GPS unit is handy) and submit your findings to the county archaeology dept and/or a museum. You will find there are various coin registers e.g. http://info.ox.ac.uk/~archinfo/ccindex/

Mud-larking below high tide on the River Medway.

ccindex.htm which is the gateway to the Celtic coin register at The Institute of Archaeology, 36 Beaumont Street. Oxford.

Warning: if you ever go mudlarking on rivers or the sea shore do not go alone! Mud, tides and slippery stones can be quite treacherous!

8. AERIAL PHOTOGRAPHY: I think this is one of the most important modern tools for discovering new sites and studying the wider concepts of known ones. One does not have to go flying, for there are a great many collections of aerial photographs for you to study. Phone or write to your

Field walking a Roman villa in Sussex. Comparing finds.

Junct. 8/M20. Area of the Iron Age pots (see page 116).

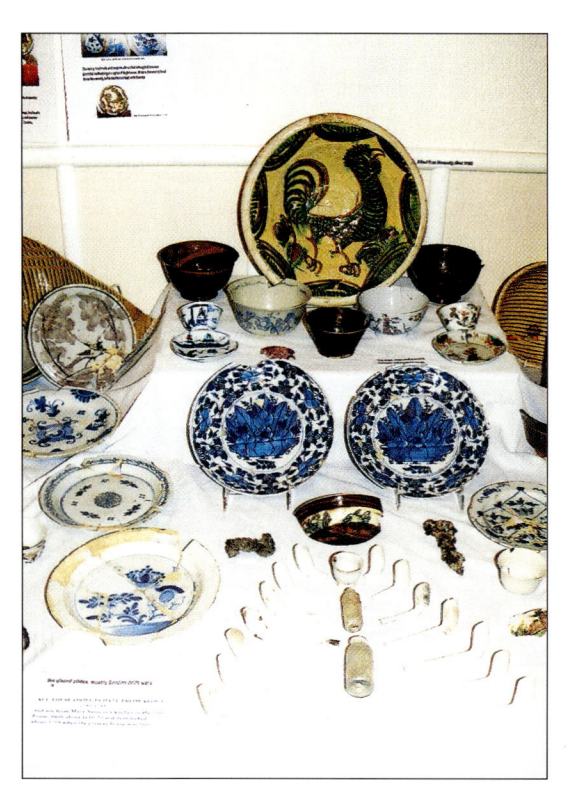

county archives or the Royal Commission on the Historical Monuments at Swindon (now part of English Heritage) or to Cambridge University Committee for Photography, they will all provide access to their aerial photographs. There are plenty of books on the subject (e.g. *"Aerial Archaeology in Britain"* …Shire Series) so familiarise yourself as to how and why features show as crop marks. Sometimes it is only one day that things will show as a crop ripens unevenly and reveals shadows of what is beneath. Here is a photograph (oblique not vertically overhead) of the M20/junction 8 site that had the Iron Age settlement. The shadowy structure in the foreground has now all but disappeared under the new railway. The pots were found off the top section (beyond the curved road) the entrance to the I.A. settlement was probably the pitchfork shaped road of Musket Lane (now all gone).

9. BACK-YARD ARCHAEOLOGY: if you have a back-yard that is your own property there is often scope for a small scale excavation and you might be surprised at what you find! Before you start learn how to do an excavation properly, perhaps go on several other digs first to learn the ropes. Here are photographs of the 2000 Centenary dig in Hastings at 5, High Street. There were several 18th-19th century household rubbish pits yielding a remarkable collection of superb items. I can remember washing the 'cockerel' plate and am amazed that all its pieces were eventually found! H.A.A.R.G. members did most of the digging, recording, drawing etc.

The owner, a well known professional archaeologist will shortly be writing and publishing a report on all the finds and the history of the house. It certainly was an excellent "backyard dig" and everyone thoroughly enjoyed it!

Some of this imported 17th - 18th century pottery particularly the French 'Cockerel' plate could have been smugglers contraband. Many of the Hastings residents were involved in smuggling and it is known an 18th century owner of the house had connections to the 'trade'.

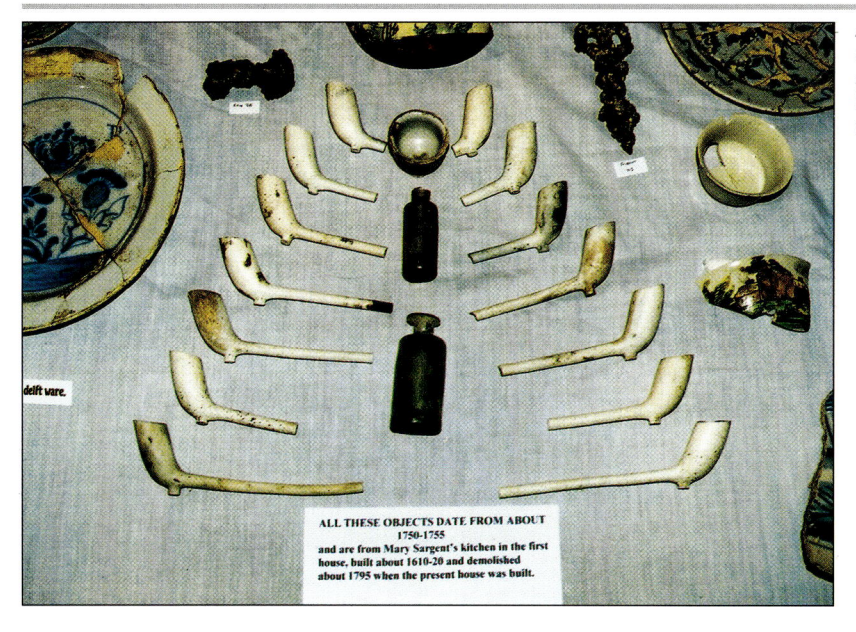

A selection of 18th century Churchwarden clay pipes. Their stems would originally have been longer but it is unusual to find such a good collection.

ALL THESE OBJECTS DATE FROM ABOUT 1750-1755 and are from Mary Sargent's kitchen in the first house, built about 1610-20 and demolished about 1795 when the present house was built.

One of the people I met down in Sussex when I was on course there had an allotment in Chichester and every week he came in with yet another amazing item he had found there. So get digging at home ….but make sure the gardener of the household is willing before you start uprooting the petunias!

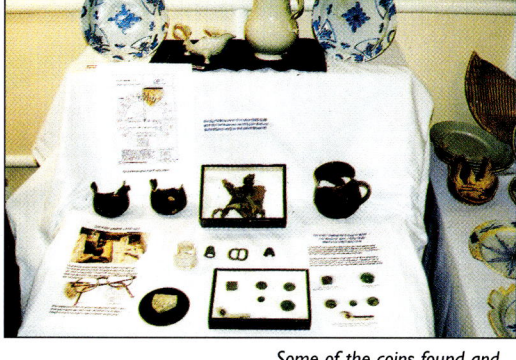

Some of the coins found and blue and white Delft china.

Collection of 18th century plates.

Wine bottles and kitchen crockery circa 1757.

Trosley Church (written on maps as Trottiscliffe) dedicated to Saints Peter and Paul, nestles under the Downs with a quiet air of peace and simplicity. It is difficult to do justice to that amazing aura but the above painting is my vain attempt to capture it in watercolour. All of the sub-downland churches in Kent (astride the spring line) have a similar serenity.

Clues as to how the vernacular pronunciation differs so dramatically from the written spelling are unclear. I favour a French connection 'Trois-des-Clefs". The "f" being silent, and doubling in medieval script with the "s", 'trois' became 'troz', so both names survived parallel. Were the three clefs ley lines ....or long barrows? Strange that it is dedicated to Peter, the keeper of the keys, and even stranger coincidence that two of the south windows are dedicated to the Key family. The north window has a very old depiction of the sun and moon, it dates from around 1342.

Half a mile east towards the rising sun (or moon) is Coldrum, once looking down a sarsen corridor to Kit's Coty. But Coldrum is not visible from the church being over a substantial hill ....so was there another long barrow looking west from that ridge (not such a 'holy' direction for the early Saxon Christians) and was it dismantled? Sarsens were used as foundations of the church ...where they still lie, some half dozen, for all to see.

The three keys ....suppose there was another barrow looking out from the hill due south ....is it still there but sealed and buried? Or does the Chestnuts, one mile due south, represent that third 'clef' in the story?

But it is a story; the late Archbishop of Canterbury, Robert Runcie, once said in a homily:-

"I am sitting in the crypt of Lambeth, a dark and secret place that holds up the whole church."

One can only puzzle as to whether he hinted some profound meaning to his words for there are some who believe that Christ knew the esoteric, mystical importance of the mystery religions. So were the legends correct? DID Christ come to England in his youth to learn and discuss the secrets of the universe, astronomy and geomagnetism, with the Celtic sages? was there an ancient Golden Age of Peace and Knowledge, an ancient Megalithic civilisation that came from the west .... beyond the setting sun, a lost Atlantis? O.K. you scoffers! If you are so sure that I am wrong why has the great number of huge long barrows in the Medway Valley (greater than anywhere else in Europe) never even been logged/investigated completely (including the slighted ones)? If anyone of you thinks I am talking rubbish go out and prove those barrows were _not_ important and were _not_ set in any particular plan then I might believe you!

One must keep an open mind (else the brain becomes a walnut) knowledge is infinite and we have forgotten what once existed ....and still exists.

Chapter 16

Afterthoughts or the Eadish

The title of this chapter is an old word meaning the 'growing grass after mowing'. So is the appreciation of our heritage going to grow after so much has been 'mown' by highway and rail development? one would hope so. E.A.D. also stands in my way of thinking as epitaph and denouement …the outcome of events!

I can only wonder at the type of person who is reading/read this book. I suppose my real aim I had in mind when writing it was educational - to show people what a wealth of archaeology and 'lost' heritage abounds under the fields of Kent and Britain, there to be discovered assessed and recorded. Not necessarily dug (which in some cases destroys) but to be preserved, understood and respected (not ploughed to smithereens in oblivion). *A nation that does not respect and learn from its past loses its future.* (Not my words but adapted from others).

"What does it matter to us?" some might say, but how lacking in foresight they are! Apart from a wealth of yet undiscovered sites there are in actual fact two major finds that if found would draw people to Britain in droves to see them, two lost treasures that have never been located. King John's treasure lost in the quicksands of Norfolk (now dry land) and Boadicea's grave. King John's treasure probably lies in the vicinity just north of Holbeach. One can try and work it out from historical records of where the Wash and crossing used to be. His caravan probably went too far north and the guides mistook the villages and features they had to head for across the bay. One day someone will find those cart loads of treasure and I hope it is an unpaid (amateur) archaeologist working with ground radar or a good scope that takes the credit. Maybe it is in someone's back garden!

Boadicea, presents an even greater, far wider, problem. Where did she flee to? Where was the last battle? No one knows for sure.

My discovery of the possible 'Horse of the Hesperis' and the theory evolving from that, namely that the ancient Celts looked upon the landscape as sacred and akin to the stars, gave me a jolt. A jolt back to thoughts I had long ago in my childhood. We lived, till I was seven, near Bexley in north Kent and many times travelling towards London through the Crown Woods on Shooters Hill, I had this extraordinary urge to shout out *"Stop the car, I want to get out and walk through there"*! Perhaps it was the beautiful birches and bracken, particularly striking in the golden autumn tones, that attracted me. It was not till I was adult that I remember actually walking part of that forest as it stretches down to Abbey Wood …….the Abbey itself has a haunting quiet, peace (at least it has to my perceptions) and this links into thoughts I have had since I first read about the last battle of the ancient Celts.

It is supposed (by the historians) that after sacking Londinium as it was called, Boadicea led her troops northwards to a battle somewhere north of Watford! …..but always in my imagination it was not so ….my mental picture of that horrendous slaughter has always been on the high ground of Shooter's Hill, **south** of the Thames! 90,000 Celts were killed or so we are told …that is a heck of a lot to bury and their graves (with so few Celts left to do the honours) would likely have been close to where they fell. Abbey Wood is just two miles from Shooters and there is a barrow marked on the modern map so it was a sacred burial place. Is that mysterious peace of the Abbey partly an emotion from a preceding cataclysm? Did the monks sense something also that caused them to build it in that place?

> "Is it illusion?or does there a spirit from perfecter ages, Here, even yet, amid loss, change, and corruption, abide?
> Is it illusion that lures the barbarian stranger, Brings him with gold to the shrine, brings him in arms to the gate?"
> Arthur Hugh Clough

I have not researched the archaeological record for that area but came across one very strange account in George Payne's book written in 1893. He reprinted an earlier description of finds in Claylane Woods that was written in the *Gentleman's Magazine* of 1846. (Claylane is 12 miles further down Watling Street from Shooter's Hill and the wood is still there). The extract is as follows:-

"In 1825 some labourers while grubbing up a piece of Claylane Wood came upon an entrenchment, in the centre of which they discovered at the very least three waggon loads of human bones, mingled with leather, many metal celts, spear-heads, and armour, the latter in such preservation that a suit was actually put on by one of the labourers. The bones were collected and thrown into the surrounding fosse; the earth which formed the vallum was then thrown over them and the soil levelled. Some of the celts, several portions of the armour, and pieces of the weapons are preserved in the Museum of Gravesend. The armour was taken to Cobham Hall by the finders, who expected a noble reward for their pains, but the then noble owner, being no archaeologist, ordered the men some refreshment and told them to take their rubbish away. After this rebuff, and knowing no collectors of antiquities, they sorted out the metal, and after breaking it into pieces sold above a bushel of it to Mr. Troughton, late Mayor of Gravesend. So bright was the metal that one of the celts was actually tested by fire to see if it was not gold, and still bears the mark of this illusage." George Payne goes on to say that: *"From Mr. Roach Smith's note-book for 1842 I learn that some of the celts were in the possession of Mr. Crafter of Gravesend. Should the remaining portion of Claylane Wood ever be grubbed (as we hope it may) there is no doubt that some further light would be thrown on this extraordinary discovery."*

From the modern map of the area it can clearly be seen that the wood is still there …so George Payne's words are still waiting to prove the point. BUT even as I write this the map of Kent seems now out of date. I have just been given rumour that the new M2 widening may have slashed this exact area. Word has it that the archaeology near Cobham has not been given the justice it deserves ….I just hope that is not true ……

If you look carefully at the map you will notice the closeness of Cuxton (ancient river crossing), just 6 miles distant. Perhaps the warriors were from the Battle of the Medway and slain Celts from Caratacus' army rather than from Shooter's Hill. It is doubtful the difference in years between the battle dates,

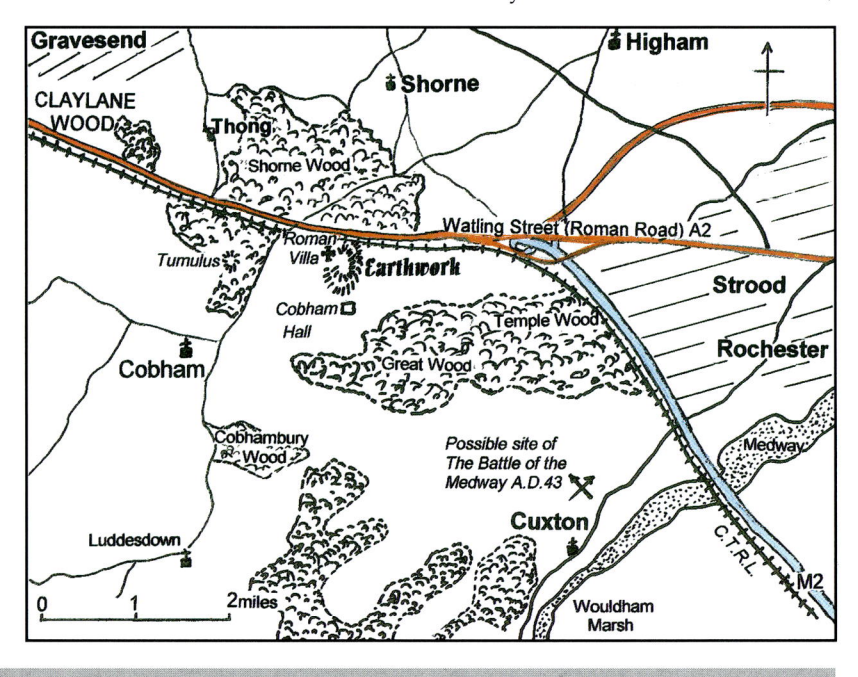

Map of the Cuxton - Gravesend area. The Cobham earthwork is mentioned in chapter 8.

A.D. 43 and A.D.60, would have much affect on the preservation of the leather, it is amazing that it survived some 2000 years at all! What also is extraordinary is that the celts (axes) were not of iron ... but from the description were bronze! This might suggest that Iron Age Celts had kept (or preferred to make) ceremonial bronze weapons of war rather than iron. (Iron ones would have presumably have rusted away). Either these were not Iron Age Celts warriors at all but were some 3000 years old and of the Bronze Age, or the presence of any bronze axes on I.A. sites has to be looked at in a different way ....possibly as heirlooms from a previous age and some 'Bronze Age' sites may actually be I.A.?

In October 1999 the Sussex Archaeological Society held a conference based on the new fangled theory that the main Roman invasion took place through Chichester, Sussex, and not through Richborough, Kent! It is a theory that I cannot believe at all! Why, for starters, would the Romans have risked shipping 5000 cavalry on a long haul trip (over 20 hours and 2 tides) to Chichester? Why later did the Romans build a triumphal arch at Richborough?

But at that conference Professor Martin Henig from Oxford stated that he thought Boadicea's last battle was **south** of the Thames and that she intended to *"take the long straight road to Chichester"*.

So, Professor Henig is the first scholar I have ever heard make the suggestion the battle **was indeed south** of the Thames. Logistically if she had intended to win against the Romans and defeat them entirely she would have planned to sack the main port, which is usually accepted to have been <u>Richborough</u>.... down the long straight road of **Watling Street** .....from Shooter's Hill! (But more likely along the safer Celtic route of 'Old street' that leads past Woodstock.)

So, does all this make sense and link into my theory that the main sacred 'temple' area of the Iron Age Celts was in Kent? Kent was arguably the most densely populated Celtic area. Perhaps Boadicea intended to head into Kent, the major stronghold of the Catuvellauni, to gather support and sack Richborough. But then after the disastrous defeat ....fled that way anyway ...to the temple. After all, she would have been the wrong side of the Thames to flee back to East Anglia and Iceni country .....and she was supposedly the personification of the horse goddess, Epona .

Things would appear to fit this scenario.

What I have just explained opens up an entirely new possibility never mentioned in scripts before, (as far as I know) and would infer that her burial place is in Kent and most likely <u>IF</u> my theories are correct ...within the square/constellation of Pegasus! Is her grave near the centre, near St. Catherine's church? or at Lewson Street, = the *Lady's Stone or the Mistress's mound* or in the 'heart' of the horse at Newbury? Or in its head at Barrow Green? There are several possibilities, but it is likely that the grave would have been demarked by a rectangular ditch in Iron Age fashion ...so that is what to look for. There was a rectangular ditch at the Highsted grave site (look back and see). Would it be possible that the supposition she had a regal grave be incorrect and that few grave goods were included? This gets back immediately to the mysterious theft ....were there any items that were unique and valuable that we were not told about?

Having dropped in these further possibilities, I hope a few more budding archaeologists are inspired to look for Iron Age enclosures. I know of two sites that are the right size and shape never investigated or recorded. Yet another rectangular shadow appears on an aerial photograph recently shown at a Kent lecture and no one in the audience remarked on it!

For those mainly interested in Romans, there are dozens of villa farms to be located. The string north of Watling street have mostly been located (recent good work done by Dr. Paul Wilkinson) but there should be a chain further south, spreading west from Little Newbury (excavated by B. Philp 1985) Pitstock (aerial, ground evidence) and Highsted Farm (tile and pottery evidence) which are all lying one Roman mile apart. The series could then be predicted roughly all the way west to the known Villa site at Hartlip:-

Hartlip RV → Chesley → Danaway → Eyehorn Hatch → **Sutton Baron** (Borden) → Tunstall → Highsted → Pitstock- → **Newbury RV**

Another series 2 miles futher south than that is likely to be :-

Deans Bottom → Silver Street → Bexon → Milstead → Great Higham → Down Court → Doddington

And south of the Downs yet another line that may or may not exist:-

Eccles RV → Boxley → Detling → **Thurham RV** → Water Lane → Broad Street → Hollingbourne → Greenway Crt → Harrietsham

I may be surmising too much on this …but I do not think so somehow! It is likely there are even more!! Just get out there and look (the right way remember) and then perhaps get the sites 'geophysed' and recorded. I have spotted another possible R.V. on an aerial photograph south of Thurnham on the banks of the River Len.

Just north of there was a very large Iron Age settlement that was destroyed by the rail track. More archaeology <u>could</u> have been done for I realised that there were pots still sticking out of the sand! But sadly although some were rescued and the archaeology 'completed', the rest were bulldozed. The official line was:- *"We have aimed therefore to open up as extensive areas as possible and investigate "settlement dynamics"…….is it more important to excavate a few more pots or to get a better understanding of a site's archaeology and its relationship to other sites along the CTRL?"*

This is a very valid statement but from what I had found, in getting enough evidence to alert both the Kent Archaeological Society President and the County Archaeologist, was that these pots being left behind were all individual and unique. They appeared to be late Iron Age cooking pots placed upside down in a cooking trench, complete with square pot boilers and remains of food. So would study of these pots in detail have revealed a lot more about the relationship of this site to Kent itself? I think it would, for it could even have been a site hastily abandoned before the advancing Roman invasion force. Was the Len Valley the most important Iron Age area in Kent?

Still, I suppose its destruction was fate, for it seems to have been predicted by Lewis Carroll in his nonsense poem *"The Hunting of the Snark"* for the high point near the site is Snarkhurst Wood:-

Late Iron Age pots, in the sand near Snarkhurst, Hollingbourne. Many like these were abandoned to the bulldozer.

"They sought it with thimbles, they sought it with care
They pursued it with forks and hope;
*They threatened its life with a **railway-share**;*
They charmed it with smiles and soap."

Just a few miles down the road lie Lenham and Harrietsham. The position of Lenham itself is interesting as it is the source of the Len and the Stour…one flowing east the other west. It is equidistant between Ashford and Maidstone (known Roman centres) also about eight miles from Faversham. So is the large amount of archaeology near Harrietsham church part of a large Roman town? Why should Harrietsham Parish Council not be given Euopean Union funding to help them do the archaeology if they really need a new school on that site? It could be extremely important indeed in helping to prove the importance of the area.

Apparently Kent is helping do some archaeology in Northern France to help get funding from the EU to do work back in England ….if you can work that one out you are far brighter than me ….it has flummoxed me! One only hopes that British archaeology does not allow the E.U. to exclude unpaid archaeologsts on digs (as they often insist on the continent), surely Britain can lead Europe for a change, particularly in aspects of archaeology?

In the 17th century John Speed marked the strange name of 'Durolenum' on one edition of his 1611 map (it disappeared from the other editions) so was **his naming actually correct? Was there a Roman garrison town between these villages? The most likely place to look for it is Dickley Wood (meaning 'ditched').**

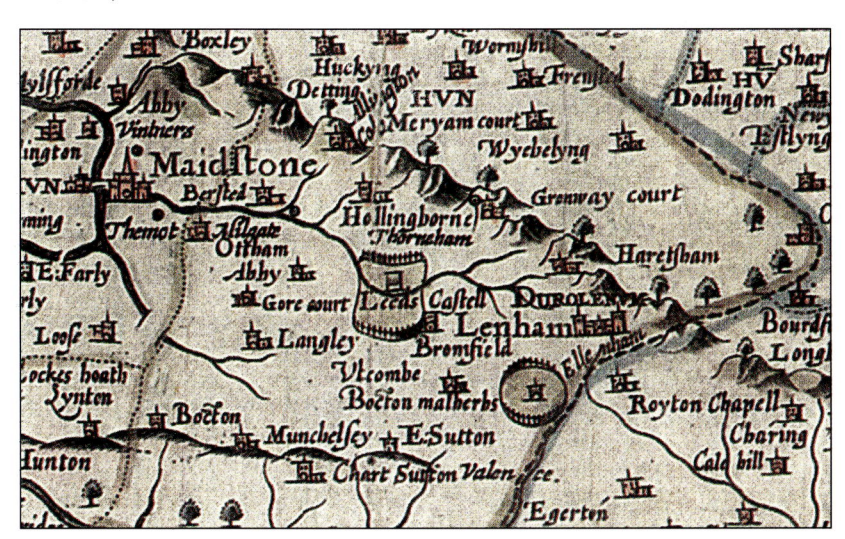

Throughout this book I have tried to inspire people to look for, record, and investigate archaeology. Sadly I feel the subject in Kent is like a Trojan Horse, hollow because much of it is excavated and taken out of the county … and we as a county have almost been betrayed! At the time of writing this (26.6.2001) there is no <u>central</u> Archaeological Trust/Unit to do investigative archaeology and tender for contracts such as the recent Channel Tunnel Rail Link. Most of those contracts went to out of county units such as Oxford and Wessex. Why cannot businessmen and county authorities organise a unit to fill this vast empty space in a subject that is fast grabbing people's interest? …..for we, who should have the richest amount of pre-history in the country, have perhaps the least to show for it! So I finish this book much as I started, restating that archaeology should be of interest to all and ideally there should be this central Kent Archaeological Unit to which farmers/metal detectorists/everyone can go for help, advice and immediate assistance for all finds/data.

One last afterthought: I like to turn things upside down and look at things with fresh eyes. If the Celts were in fact dyslexic (not willing to write things down and could not tell their right hands from their left) what if someone confused west and east? …..and it got confused in the writing? One sentence of the Bible stood on end in this way makes an incredible effect on how we might see things *"And there came wise men from the west …."* It would in fact make sense. It is FACT that Kent has the largest and most numerous Megalithic long barrows in Europe …its just that they have mostly been slighted. It is FACT that the Neolithic genes of western British Celts (Welsh) are proving to be extremely old. What if the astronomical knowledge of those ancient people was way beyond the rest of Europe? After all the long barrows are older in many cases than the pyramids. What if the cultural centre of ancient Celts was in Britain and certain things spread eastwards …and not the other way around?

Eadish could be food for thought, and hope it will leave you thinking about things!

Further Reading ...a short list

Kentish archaeology:-

Ashbee, Paul, *The Medway's Megalithic Long Barrows*. In *Archaeologia Cantiana. Vol. 120*. Kent Arch. Soc., and *The Medway Megaliths in a European Context*. Vol 119, 1999

Guy, John, *Kent Castles*. Mereborough 1980.

Jay, Len, *Thanet Beakers*. Monograph pub. by the Trust for Thanet Archaeology 1994

Journal of Canterbury Archaeology Trust *"Canterbury's Archaeology"* on going publication.

Payne, George, *Collectiana Cantiana, Archaeological researches in the Neighbourhood of Sittingbourne & other parts of Kent*. London 1893.

Margary, I. D., *Roman Ways in the Weald*. Phoenix House 1948.

Peddie, John, *The Roman Conquest of Britain*. Alan Sutton 1987.

Wallenberg, J. K., *Kentish Place Names* and *Place Names of Kent*. Uppsala Univ. 1931

Ward, Gordon, *Belgic Britons, Men of Kent in B.C.55*. Caxton & Holmesdale 1961.

General archaeology/finds/sites:-

British Museum Publication 1975, *Flint Instruments*.

Champion, Timothy (et al) *Prehistoric Europe*. Academic Press 1984.

Cunliffe, Barry, (et al) *Prehistoric Europe, An Illustrated History*. Oxford 1998.

Cunliffe, Barry, (et al) *Ancient Celts*. Oxford 1997.

Gibson, Alex and Woods, Ann, *Prehistoric Pottery for the Archaeologist*. Leicester Univ. Press 1990.

Riley, D. N., *Aerial Archaeology in Britain*. Shire Archaeology 1982.

See Also - **Shire Archaeology** booklets on various subjects & English Heritage series:- **Stone Age Britain, Bronze Age Britain, Iron Age Britain.**

Enigmas/standing stones/astronomy:-

Aveni, Anthony, *Nasca, Eighth Wonder of the World?* British Museum 2000.

Bond, Frederick, Bligh, *The Gate of Rememberance*. Oxford. Basil Blackwell 1918.

Bord, Janet and Colin, *Mysterious Britain*. Garnstone 1972.

Castleden, Rodney, *The Wilmington Giant, the quest for a lost myth*. Turnstone 1983.

Brennan, Martin, *The Stars and the Stones*. (about Newgrange). Thames & Hudson 1983.

Robbins, Don, *Circles of Silence*. Souvenir Press 1986.

Service, Alastair and Bradbery, Jean, *The Standing Stones of Europe*. Weidenfeld & Nicholson 1979.

Szekely, Edmond, *Gospel of the Essenes*. Daniel 1974.

Tirion, Wil, *Cambridge Star Atlas 2000*.

Coastal/marshland connections:-

Cooper, W. D., *Winchelsea*. East Sussex County Library 1986.

Eddison, Jill, *Romney Marsh, survival on a frontier*. Tempus 2000.

O'Sullivan, Aidnan, *The Archaeology of Lake Settlement in Ireland*. Discovery Prog. Monograph 4, Royal Irish Academy 1998.

Countryside/woodlands/wildlife:-

Brimble, L. J. F., *Trees in Britain*. McMillan 1948.

Godet, Jean-Denis, *Trees & Shrubs of Great Britain & Northern Europe*. Mosaik 1993/Collins 1988.

Marren, Peter, *The Wild Woods, a regional guide to Britain's ancient woodland*. Nature Conservancy Council 1992.

Rackham, Oliver, *History of the Countryside*. J. Dent 1986.

Roberts, Geoffrey, *Woodlands of Kent*. Geerings 1999.

Art and drawing:-

Edwards, Betty, *Drawing on the Right Side of the brain*. Souvenir Press 1981.

Griffiths, Nick, Jenner, Anne and Wilson, Christine, *Drawing Archaeological Finds. - A Handbook*. Archetype Pub. 1990

Index

Unless otherwise specified, place names refer to Kent. Material in pictures and captions rather than running text is in italics.

Abbey Wood (Greenwich) 113
aerial photographs 109-10
   Highsted *2*
Allen, Don 15, 16
Allen, Hugh 16, *18*
ancient sites, fragility 49-50
archaeology
   nature of 89
   and New Age beliefs 91
ash trees, and Hollow Way 69
   Associated Portland Cement Manufacturers (A.P.C.M. Ltd) 15, 16, 17, 61
astronomy 39, 93, *94*, 96-97, 102
Atlantis 76
auger hole investigations 47
badger 64, 70-71, 72
banks and ditches, importance 24, 26, 41, *42*, 46
Barker, Peter 95
Barling (Essex) 81
Barrow Green 98
Bartlett, Alister 47, 51, 75
Bartlett-Clark Consultancy 47
Batemans (East Sussex) 81
Bath, Somerset 98
Battle of the Medway 114-15
Beaker remains 15, 47, *49*, 57
Beckley (East Sussex) *107*
Belgic remains 15, 25, 47, *48*, 57
Berry, A.N. 15
Berry, H. 16, 17
Bethersden *30*, 84
Binbury 80-81, 104
birch 61
Birch, Dr R.G. *18*, 43
Bloomstein, Miss M. 16
Blue Bell Hill *32*, 35, 60, 101
   and CTRL 91, 104-5
Boadicea, grave 113, 115
Bond, Frederick 90-91
Boxley 31, *32*
Brimble, L.J.F. 65
Bronze Age 25, 35-37, 59, 101
bronze axe(s) *2*, 26, 57, 115
   Kent finds 26, 47, *49*, 53, 57
   see also Celts, ancient
Bumpits, Lynsted 96
burial rites, worldwide comparisons 80
burnet moth 71-72
Burns, Robert 89

butterflies 71, 72
Cambridge University, resources 109-10
Canterbury 80
Canterbury Archaeology Trust 22, 25
Carnac (Brittany) 81, 82
Castle Toll 104
cats, properties 77
Celts, ancient 29, 44, 77, 80, 117
    and astronomy/astrology 93, 103
    see also Bronze Age; Iron Age; Neolithic Age
chalk, and drinking water 40
chalk cemetery 15-20
    theft at 15-16
Chalk Pits 61-64
Channel Tunnel Rail Link (CTRL) 117
    and Blue Bell Hill 91, 104-5
    and Iron Age finds 110, 116
chariot burial 96
Chatham 96
chestnut 69
Chichester (West Sussex) 115
cinnabar moth *71*
circles, stone *100*, 101-103
Claylane Woods 114
climate, differences 57
Cobham 59, 114
coin registers 108-9
coins 67, 95-96
Coldrum Barrow 85, *86*, 101, 112
compass points, significance 35
constellations 88, 93-94, 99, 102
Copper Age 59
courses, for amateurs 108
Cox, David 53
cranogs 104
cremation 15
crop marks 97
Cunliffe, Barry 43, 98
Curran, Clare 44, 47, *51*
Cuxton 114
Detling 80-81, 83, 104
Devon, Bronze Age layout 35-37
diagonals 92
Doddington *28*, *100*, 102, 103
Doubleday, Garth 21, 41
Dover boat 25, 66
dowsing *40*, 47, 74-75
dreams, and energy 91-92
drinking water, availability 40
Dungeness 83, 84
durmast 64-67
Durolenum 117
dyslexia 29, 117
East Kent Gazette 16, 17
Eastling 83, *100*, 102, 103
Ebbsfleet 88, 89

electricity, effect of static 73-75, 91
energy, and dreams 91-92
Epona 97, 115
Eppilus, coins find 95-96, 102
Fairlight 104
Feakes, David 15, 16, *18*, 21
fertility symbol *87*
field maple 67, *68*, 70
field walking 108
Fishbourne (West Sussex) 83
flints 25
   finds
      Woodstock 22-23, *23-24*, 48, 54, 57
         in tumulus 55, 56, 80
   natural nodules 87
fox 64
France 81, 82
Freemasons 81, 89, 98
Frinsted 95, *98*, 103
genetic predisposition 79
geode stones 43, 57
geophysics 47, 53, 75
ghosts *77*
Gillingham Coroner 43
glass 53-54, 57, 60
Glassenbury 82
Glastonbury (Somerset) 90-91
Glossam's Place, E. Sussex 107
Global Positioning System (GPS) 9, 108
Goldsmith, Eric 66
graves 57
graves, burnt 16, 17
Great Square of Pegasus 93-94, *94*, 95-100, 103, 115
green woodpeckers 70
Greenhalgh, Michael *106*
grog (see pot sherds)
Guy's Hospital (London) 16, 19
Half Mile Path 79, 80
Halley's comet 98
Harrietsham 75, 91, 116
Hastings Area Archaeology Group (HAARG) 45, 107
Hastings (East Sussex) *106*, 110-11
Hawkenbury 82
Hawkins, Alastair *51*
Hawkins, Alison 20, 21
Hawkins, Elinor *10*, 22, 24
Heaslip, Matthew *59*
Henig, Martin 115
Hesperis, meaning 97
Highsted *2*, 9, 93
   banks *46*
   detailed plan *8*
   reconstruction *58*
   site map *12*
   surveying *59*
   see also Woodstock

Highsted River, map *39*
Hinduism, parallels with 97, 98
Hollingbourne 60, 116
Hollow Way 54, 60, 69
home ground, archaeological possibilities 110
hornbeam 69
Horse of the Hesperis 93-94, *94*, 95-100, 103, 115
horses 96-97, 99
horse & cart burial 5
horseshoe *27*
Hubbard, Harry 16, *18*
Impton Wood 101-2
interment 15
internet, use of 41
Invicta horse 98, 99
iron 90
Iron Age 45, 59, 96, 101
    Woodstock 15, 22, *27*, 41, 53, 57, 59, 60
    see also Celts, ancient
Iron Age pots *116*
    Woodstock 25, 53
iron ingot, significance 60
iron slag 22, *23*, 26, 57, 60
Jay, Len 41
Jeakes, Samuel 85
Jesus, travels in youth 97, 112
John the Baptist, St 103
John, King, lost treasure 113
Julliberie's Grave 85
Kelly, David 15
Kent, map *13*
Kent Archaeological Society 15, 16, *106*, 116
Kingsdown 92-93
Kipling, Rudyard 78, 81, 89
Kit's Coty *78*, 85, *86*
La Tene III brooch 15, *19*
land owners, permission from 107-8
landscape, sacred nature of 97
Len Valley 116
Lenham 45, *100*, 116, 117
Leo of Thanet 88, 99
Les Alignements 82
Lewson Street 98
leylines 35
Lidsing 83
lightning, and oak trees 67
lion, and Isle of Thanet 88
Little Newbury 27, 97, 116
local archaeological societies 60
Long Man of Wilmington 81
loop and socket axe 26
Lower Medway Archaeological Research Group (L.M.A.R.G.) 53, 101
Lynsted 93, 96, 98
magnetism 74-75, 79-81, 91
Maidstone Area Archaeology Group (M.A.A.G.) 47
Maidstone Museum 15, 16, 19

Malta 99, 105
maple, field 67, *68*, 70
Margary, Ivan 29
mechanical excavation, use of 53
medieval period, and remains 25, 101
mediums, use 76
Medway, Battle of the 114-15
Medway Valley 101, 112
Megalithic sites 101
Mesolithic Age 22, *23-24*, 57, 59, 104
metal detection 21-22, 108
Milstead 67
mint, possible location 102-3
mistletoe, in Kent 67-68
Mithras, stone 31
Moatenden 82-83
moats 55, 59, 60
modern times, and sarsens 101
Mohawk Indians 79
moles 22
moths 71-72
mudlarking, for amateurs 109
Neolithic Age 22, *23-24*, 48, 57, 59, 101
   longhouse 91
   pottery *48*
   see also Celts, ancient
New Age beliefs 91
Newenden 104
Newington 31
Newnham 93, 96, *100*
oak 64-65
Old Street, and Boadicea 115
orchards, grubbing 21, 23, 24
orchids 62-63
Ordnance Survey
   1909 map *10, 100,* 102
   modern map *11*
Pack, Archie 16
Page, Arthur 19, 20
parch marks 50, 53
Parisii Celts 96
particle physics 75-76
Patel, Beena 24, 47, *51*
Patel, Sunita *10*
Payne, George 13, 21, 30, 35, 38, 55-56, 93, 114
Pegasus *see* Great Square of Pegasus
Perkins, David 20, 51, 96
Philp, Brian 27, 97, 116
Pitstock Farm 11, 27
place names, significance 83
plough banks 41, *42*, 48, 57
Pluckley 77
Ponton, D.T.A. 16, 17, *18*, 19
Postling 83
pot sherds, significance 44-45
   grog ware 25, 47, *48*, 57, 83

pottery, finds 57
Quercus petraea 64-66
rabbits 63
ragwort 72
reading, for amateurs 108
reaves 37, 77
recording finds, for amateurs 108
Reculver 88, 89
research, for amateurs 108
resistivity surveys 51, *106*
Ringlestone 103
rivers, importance 38
road building, Romans 29
Robbins, Don 103
Rodmersham 65-66, *87*, 97
Roman remains 27, 29, 30, 101, 116
　　finds 47, *49*, 53-54, 57
Romney Marsh 83
Royal Commission on the Historical Monuments (Swindon) 109-10
Royal Scottish Museum 15
Runcie, Robert 112
Rutherford, J.R. 16, *18*
Rye (East Sussex) 83, 84
sacred trees 66-67
sacrifice 98
sarsens 31, *32*, 38, 101
Saxons, use of earlier roads 29
sea, importance 38
sea level, and climate 57
Seaford Head (East Sussex) 81
Seed 96, *100*
settlements, and water 37-38
sheep, and Sheppey 87-88, 99
Sheppey, Isle of, and sheep 87-88, 99
Shooter's Hill (Greenwich) 115
Silbury Hill 81
sling shots 43, 57
SMR sites, and metal detection 108
Snarkhurst *116*
Speed, John, 1611 map 117
Stalisfield Green 103
Stevens, Martin 16, *18*
Stone-in-Oxney 31, 84
Stonehenge, sacred nature 97
straight walking 79
sun, as primary source of matter 90
Sussex, archaeology in 45
Sussex Archaeological Society 45, 115
Sussex University 51, 53
Tester, P.J. 59
Teynham Street 98
Thanet, Isle of 88, 99
Thurnham 80-81
Timbold Hill 93, 95
time, as fourth dimension 91
Tincommius 95

Tonge *37*, 38, 40, 103
totem poles 80
Trackway Map 29, 33, *34*
trackways 29-37, 77
trees, sacred 66-67
Trottiscliffe 85, *86*, 112
tumuli 80-81
Twopenny, Edward 13, 55
Uffington Horse 99
Valetta Convention 105
Van der Graaf generators 73-74
Verica, coins find 95-96, 102
Walderslade 101-2
walnut 61
water 40, 57, 91
waterways 37-40
White Horse Stone 91
wildlife 61-72
Wilkinson, Paul 97, 98, 116
Wilmington, Long Man of (East Sussex) 81
Winchelsea (East Sussex) 83-85
Windover Hill (East Sussex) 81
Winter, Frederick 16
woodpecker, green 70
Woodstock *8*, 9, 25-26, 60
  digs
    1955 15-20
      theft of artefacts 15
    1996 47-51
      Trench I *50, 52*
        finds 47-48
      Trench II, finds 47
    1998 *52*, 53-56
  map
    1909 *10*
    modern *11*
  see also Highsted
Woodstock House *9*
Wright, Thomas 85
Wychling 30, 31, *32*, *33*, 83, 85
yaffle 70
Yorkshire 96